The Alternative Wrong: Unbinding from Toxic Culture

The Alternative Wrong

Ryan Starbloak

Cover art by Pinky Inoturan

Edited by Rogena Mitchell-Jones

Visit my website at:
www.ryansleavitt.com/starbloak

Also by **Ryan Starbloak:**

Freckles Over Scars
GOD & everything
First Reality
This Never Happened Somewhere
Funny Looks On a Serious Face
The Alternative Wrong

As **Ryan S. Leavitt:**

Writer, Seeker, Killer

THE FELLED
Never Going Back
Pure Intention

Table of Contents

Part One: The Before……pg. 1

Part Two: The Now..… pg. 31

Part Three: The After.…. pg. 119

Source Material.…………… pg. 165

To Hannah & Quang, who shared with me a place for peace of mind, community, and the thoughts found within this book.

Part One: The Before

"Our normal waking consciousness… is but one special type of consciousness, whilst all about it, parted from it by the filmiest of screens, there lie potential forms of consciousness entirely different… No account of the universe in its totality can be final which leaves these other forms of consciousness quite disregarded."

-William James

1

"Events before the Big Bang are simply not defined, because there's no way one could measure what happened at them. Since events before the Big Bang have no observational consequences, one may as well cut them out of the theory, and say that time began at the Big Bang."

–Stephen Hawking

What you want to know and what you need to know is being kept from you.

The most troubling aspect of this lies in the fact that there isn't some big brother keeping it from you— it's you. The chances are you've probably already heard everything you've ever needed to know to live the life you want. At some point, I'm confident you felt like you had everything figured out, that some great epiphany was bestowed upon you, which, if you could embrace it, things would be excellent once and for all. As if this life was a fairy tale and you sensed a greater destiny of being chosen.

At different points in your life, you could probably identify times when you had something you wanted but not something you needed or vice versa— that "something is missing here" kind of mentality. If only it would all arrive at once and at last, right?

Picture a time where you felt in the depths of your

being precisely what you wanted to do or be, but you were discouraged by someone who you considered to be very sensible.

My hope here is to jog your memory to these moments where you felt like you nearly had it.

So what exactly is this information?

Listen, to be honest, I have no idea. What I want is for this book to be a way for you to set out to that path where meaningful and sustainable progress can be at your disposal. It's not going to be easy. Hell, you might never find out what you need. Regardless, I think you can agree it's at least *possible* for you to become the self of your dreams. People do it all the time. And I like to think the people that don't have something in common— they can't live with what they know.

This difference is our concern, and we'll be exploring many facets of this fundamental, measurable difference using the most urgent and moving methods of rationality available. This *will* occasionally include nonsense. After all, if "reason" was the key to existence, then why are dogs so happy? I mean, they don't even possess the neurological framework to laugh, and they seem better off than we are in many ways, particularly within the context of emotions. Likewise, plants seem more sympathetic and giving to other organisms than humanity.

Though you might think about yourself often, you're one of the smallest objects in the entire universe. Let's take you out of the equation to discuss everything else that preceded your big deal of an existence.

According to recent developments in physics and cosmology, it seems as though non-being once reigned supreme. The Big Bang Theory suggests this, among other things. In the present, experimentation and observation indicate the universe is expanding. Scientists have been able to study the properties of the early universe, and apparently, it was incredibly tiny. It was so teeny tiny that it was just a single point, a "singularity." This is a word denoting a thing we cannot fully explain. One thing the singularity infers is that it must have contained the properties of what became our universe and the matter within.

Then there's this competing theory of creation with a little more mystique from scientists Stephen Hawking and James Hardel. They call it the "No Boundary Proposal," where the universe never began.

According to Hawking:

"Nothing was around before the Big Bang. According to Einstein's general relativity, space and time together form a space-time continuum or manifold which is not flat, but curved by the matter and energy in it. I adopt a Euclidean approach to quantum gravity to describe the beginning of the universe. In this, ordinary real time is replaced by imaginary time, which behaves like a fourth direction of space. In the Euclidean approach, the history of the universe and imaginary time is a four dimensional curved surface, like the surface of the Earth, but with two more dimensions... the Boundary Condition of the universe is that it has no boundary... the Euclidean space-time is a closed surface without edge like the surface of the Earth. One can regard imaginary and real time as beginning at the South Pole, which is a smooth point of space-time where the normal laws of physics hold. There is nothing south of the South Pole, so there was nothing around before the Big Bang."

Okay, that was almost as dense as matter within the singularity, but the takeaway is that once, there was probably only "nothing." What is meant by "nothing" is something that cannot be quantified or elaborated upon. This makes the transition from non-being to being very challenging to explain. Perhaps there were forces from outside our early universe that triggered this baffling upgrade, but Hawking believes, from his lifelong pursuits, our emotional preference for neatly defined destiny handed down by the divine is very suspicious. Number, statistics, and data are much more reliable than superstitions. They are even more reliable than humankind's imagination— what we *want* to be the case is never more potent than what is.

I think these things are worth mentioning because where we come from will inform where we are going. And if there's a false belief in that regard, our path may be an unsavory one. Secular morality is now on the rise for this very reason.

Whatever it is that you believe, *being* has emerged.

Perhaps from non-being came being. That nothing became something. That certain something, in turn, had the ability to be improved. Being has shown the ability to change its qualities, either increasing or decreasing in complexity. At first, the process was automatic, but no matter how many separate entities there have been or are, the trail we've looked back on suggests somehow non-being became being. Then being became something more, namely consciousness. You descend from this enigmatic lineage of all things. Stuff that was nothing, it would seem, became *you*. Your fate, your lot in the cosmic scheme of things, whether you wish to accept it or not, is to continue driving this project forward. And not only that but to also be open to the possibility that we have no cause. We could very well be something from nothing. And as discomforting as that is to imagine, perhaps we must return to that. But maybe not.

The Comprehensive Echelons of All Stuff

Non-being --> Being --> Consciousness --> Reflective self-consciousness --> Transcendence --> Post-Humane Divinity

Any action you take in this dance is valid. Understand that beings throughout history have been driven by some evolutionary function that allowed them to become more complex, but that obtainment of increased capabilities was unconscious and stilted. The only thing impressive about this is its longevity because it has been going on as long as time. Today, some humans live as mammals, making just enough to survive, or as YouTube personality Rob Potylo would say, are "trapped in their own nightmares." Being has consequences. One must endure suffering in haphazard and unpredictable portions. Still, though, there is a small subset of others who seek to drive their own evolution forward intentionally— those who seem to wake from that dream of themselves, to be liberated from common forms of suffering.

These others possess the ability to answer the question of "Can I live with what I know?"

2

"Mind is a tool invented by the universe to see itself; but it can never see all of itself, for much the same reason that you can't see your own back (without mirrors)."

-Robert Anton Wilson

How do you think the universe operates? It's actually a pretty straightforward question because there really aren't that many options:

A. The Law of Attraction (*The Secret*)
B. The Universe Is Actively Hostile
C. The Universe Doesn't Give a Flying Fuck About You
D. I'm flexible (i.e., they all seem reasonably feasible because I've experienced them all)

Your answer to this question tells more about you than what Hogwarts House you'd be sorted in. More than a Myers-Briggs Personality Test. One of these has to describe the universe better for you than the others, so which would you pick?

If you picked A., you also have to believe in a higher power, that this reality is some kind of filtered simulation of something else that is more real. Religious? Spiritual? Maybe you don't feel comfortable naming it, but yeah, God.

If you picked B., you are what is known as a Discordian. You worship the second law of thermodynamics, who is also Eris, the Greek goddess of chaos, personified comically in the real world.

If you picked C., you actively reject both A. and B. and might like to sing along to philosopher Jean-Paul Sartre's "Existentialism Is Humanism."

If you picked D., you sure fooled me! Or maybe you should be a bit more decisive just this once.

As there are fates worse than death, this text is going to shy away from the cosmic and the metaphysical for the most part to center in on the humanistic, social, and psychological. So there is no need to wonder if we have a soul or where we go after we die... for now. That query has confounded thinkers and ramblers long enough, and it must not wholly inform how we decide to evolve ourselves in the present. Since, you know, no one really knows what happens. At least not with enough confidence to convince the rest of us. Conversely, we know a lot about life— where it's been, where it's going, and even a few hacks on how to get it where we want quicker.

That being said, what follows cannot be learned without the proper application. If you are serious about what you're after, then practice these lessons and teachings enclosed in the real world to fully understand their meaning.

At the end of every chapter, there are questions for you to reflect upon and assist in the comprehension of what I've laid out. After all, our concern is improving what we are here and now, and that is your consciousness. A maligned, undefined region from which thoughts emerged, often times unsolicited and tumultuous.

3

"All consciousness is consciousness of something."

-Jean-Paul Sartre

Consciousness is undefined because, although you can get a dictionary definition without too much difficulty, most of Plato's dialogues clarify our ignorance. Plato's work was a firm and constant reminder that we cannot define knowledge or other ideals such as justice or love or virtue. Nor can we understand the faculty that houses this entire phenomenon— consciousness. This inability to explain the meaning of concepts remains in the present day, as there is no consensus for a definition of what consciousness is. Thus the workings of the mind remain as elusive as ever despite tremendous human process since the times of the Ancient Greeks. Brain-mapping (the process of labeling and describing the parts of the brain and how they relate to one another) is underway but still has long to go before we can adequately label consciousness. Once we have that, we'll still need to figure out the why of consciousness. Is it like the sound of a motor when you turn the ignition of a car? A byproduct of having a body?

While experts are unable to agree on what exactly consciousness is, they can construct tentative models of it to understand better what it does and why.

Guerrilla ontologist Robert Anton Wilson popularized a model of consciousness first conceived by psychologist Timothy Leary. It divides consciousness into eight different programs or "circuits." To better understand the Eight-program model of consciousness, the mind must be thought of as a kind of bio-computer. An organic electronic device that contains both software and hardware, with programs that elevate its initial functioning but also houses programs that can become superfluous or harmful depending on the intentions of the initial programmers (parents, government, educational system, peers, etc.)

The first four programs have existed for a very long time, but the latter four are more recent and found only in humans specifically. This is because our brains have developed particularly elaborate structures and parts unique in nature (to our current scientific understanding). Even more programs than eight are likely to appear the farther into the future we speculate.

The Acceleration of Knowledge is the trend of exponentially increasing information. With it, new avenues for humankind to hijack their own evolution are becoming more accessible. The active and collective outreach of this blitzing information stampede could abolish greed, poverty, and ignorance.

I will briefly summarize each of the eight programs as described in Robert Anton Wilson's book *Prometheus Rising*. That book goes into vastly greater detail than I will, and so I would highly recommend that you read it.

Now there is one thing to note before I begin, and that is to address one certain criticism that could be leveled against me— is this text not simply regurgitating words of these deceased minds without adding anything new? Well, I will admit I might not have many new transformative contributions to the Eight-program model, nor do I have any particular academic distinction in the field of psychology. However, I have become overly concerned with how obscure this model has become in the present day. It is, in my mind, something everything is searching for ceaselessly. Day in and day out, we suppress our destiny to fulfill something we believe is more urgent, only to be mired in anxiety as our surroundings seem to become more conducive to misinformation and regret. In other words, I have been studying this model for years, and I'm convinced it helps people.

So, yes, for this text to work and achieve its mission, those with any familiarity with the Eight-program model of consciousness might find things they already know, but I shall discuss it only to provide context to many of my ideas established from that very starting point.

It was Alfred North Whitehead who said, "The safest general characterization of the European philosophical tradition is that it consists of a series of footnotes to Plato." This model deserves far more recognition than it has received. I believe the lack of its applications is the source of much of our present duress. My goal here is not to take credit for this model;

only to spread awareness and understanding of it to as many people as possible.

The Eight-program model of consciousness is a rather complicated thing to wrap your head around at first, particularly the last four programs, so I'm only going to share the first four for now. It helps if you are familiar with Freudian psychology, as each program initially lines up very well with Freud's stages of human development.

Historically, this model was developed in a time when Timothy Leary was in prison, so freedom was very much on his mind. Inspired by the eight limbs of yoga and the chakra system, it seems Leary wanted to create a more scientific explanation for what consciousness was, and this is what he came up with— a kind of synthesis between Eastern and Western thought. I feel the way the systems are most linked is the way one must actively practice each of the eight nodes individually before they can do any real positive change with them (even though they are all ultimately connected and interrelate to one another).

Program One
Infancy: This is the basest instinct of all organic life, namely our fight-or-flight response, which is so attuned to our environment that we cannot consciously control our body's reaction when it feels like its life is threatened. Everything a baby does is an example of Program One, and it involves moving in terms of "forward or back" (the x-axis). A mother figure is also

identified as a protector figure at this stage, even if the actual mother is no longer available— an infant will typically imprint an approximation. An example of less than ideal conditioning on the first program is an aversion to the outside world, infophobia, but also the fear that people will hurt you to the point where we do not trust anyone. We are incredibly vulnerable when in this stage, and the imprint we receive is the most difficult to adjust if it takes the world to be hostile (unless the individual in question is subject to a genuinely and consistently hostile environment— then it is understandable). Consider a puppy that thinks all things are either friendly or delicious. This is the only program that all life has in common.

Program Two

Territory: These programs correspond with evolutionary developments. So the next program comes with the advent of mammals. It is considered the ego and first becomes imprinted as a toddler. It is where we overcome gravity and gain a new dimension of up and down (y-axis). This leads to seeing where one stands in their family to imprint dominance or submissiveness. A father figure is recognized as an authority. An example of less than ideal conditioning here is depression, where the individual has become so submissive to the point where its surroundings are no longer looked after. Depressants such as alcohol activate and relate to this program.

Program Three

Rationality: This program is arguably exclusive to humankind because it is our invention of symbol systems (language), which eventually led to information transmitted through time. (Consider I can read a book that's thousands of years old, and although it most likely isn't exactly what Plato wrote down, it's close enough to have value for my life now.) It is here children first begin mapping and clearly understanding representations (z-axis, geometrically mapping 3-D on a 2-D surface). An example of less than ideal conditioning on Program Three can be seen with rhetorical politicians in any activities that lead to systemic racism. Using language, they turn people into a threat when only certain individuals within that group are dangerous.

Program Four

Morality: Here we get beyond symbol systems, mental maps and representations start concertizing ideas and structures into societies. Ideas become action and objects in the world. This program regulates rationality by way of local taboos and laws for others to follow or else (execution or exile). It activates at puberty (specifically our first sexual/ orgasmic/ mating experience) and is also where everything we consider in a *moral* or *amoral* way originates. You see the laws of nature far transcend the parameters of human morality from here on out if you fully grasp the implications of this program. As it developed, social castes were first enacted and remain to this day in the form of wealth, privilege, and royalty. An example of less than ideal conditioning on Program Four would be a shame so potent it prevented someone from healthily exploring their sexuality.

These programs are programmed by culture and society to significant effect. They can instill any value, which can then be held to as a belief or reality tunnel to an individual for life. At the same time, most any belief can be broken, improved upon, or negated on any programs, given the proper therapeutic or consciousness-changing experience.

There is a stoppage for most human beings beyond Program Four as of 2019. The reason for this that the first four programs represent a typical mammal's experience. Birth, childhood, adolescent, adulthood, and parenthood. As a species, we are currently on the precipice of moving from Program Four to Program Five. This occasionally means an individual may stumble into Program Five and beyond but be discouraged as a result. Each time we evolve onto a higher program of consciousness, the species is permanently altered.

As this cycle of life continues to play out, though more programs of consciousness both exist and are coming into greater recognition for humankind, most merely live with the programming they are given. They do not think upon them or comprehend the damage originating from conceivably faulty processes the world has employed. The underlining point here is that some take what programming they've been given and shuffle through life robotically. Then some seek to actively accelerate their "bio-programming" and evolution— they are known as metaprogrammers. They are not content with our current timetable of evolution and believe the script found in our DNA foretells everything we need to know about it. So while metaprogrammers seem to have found higher additional programs in which to dwell, most are not even aware of their existence. This majority who fumble through life are then sometimes peddlers of a toxic culture.

By toxic culture, I mean robotization. The unconscious living where years elapse and survival is all there is. That high degree of suffering is often inherited and never escaped because the individual was not given a curiosity sufficient to break out.

However, the attempt to move to a higher station of life, a better state or peace of mind can have many tragic failures. One of the greatest truisms I've ever heard comes from the philosopher Friedrich Nietzsche. It goes something like, "Art is the conversion of suffering into beauty. The process of making something ugly or useless into something powerful and good." Though he was enveloped in the process of beckoning the future into a more metaprogrammed state, he himself lost his mind in the process. A sickly man, Nietzsche devoted his life to his philosophy and writing at the expense of his health.

On top of that, he is one of the most misread and

misunderstood minds of all time. Let that be a cautionary tale for anyone who seeks to become a metaprogrammer. Reason is needed, but we must never cast away the lower functions of our consciousness; only tame them and let them work to our advantage. Fish need to swim, dogs need to walk, and we are no different in that sense. Play, socialization, and community are vital to our psychological and physiological being. But, as Nietzsche put it, we are a bridge unto the next species beyond Homo sapiens. Nietzsche was forecasting extremely far into the future and so he did not see just how fast things in the world would change. I speak most prominently of artificial intelligence and climate emergency. Whether humans are able to achieve what Nietzsche was anticipating is contingent on these two factors.

Question: (Hey, here is the interactive section of this book, as promised. I beseech you to contemplate all the questions that conclude each chapter, especially if they have not yet dawned on you. It's an arduous thing to stop the flow of the page to reflect, but I think you'll really like the outcome. And look at all that blank space below! Deface my book with your thoughts and notes, please!)

What do you think consciousness is? What's the least favorite aspect of your own consciousness? What have you ever done about it?

4

"Our sole responsibility is to produce something smarter than we are; any problems beyond that are not ours to solve."

-Ray Kurzweil

The Acceleration of Knowledge has a predicted future point in space-time many believe is imminent. This is known as the Technological Singularity, when artificial intelligence suddenly becomes more capable than the mass theoretical processing power of every human mind in existence. Everything past that point in time is unknowable until it actually happens and that's why it's also referred to as a singularity. Just as attempting to describe time before the Big Bang is meaningless, so too is making any concrete predictions about the outcome of the Technological Singularity.

Some also imagine humanity won't reach that moment, that the Technological Singularity is simply science fiction (as seen in mass media as robots taking over ala *The Terminator*) and, therefore, unworthy of discussion, at least relative to our current climate emergency.

Just as Nietzsche was a failure, so too was another attempt to move the entire world into a collective state of higher consciousness (an ideal prelude to the Technological Singularity), a peace movement that developed and blueprinted metaprogramming itself.

I'm referring to the counter-culture movement of the 1960s that is nowhere to be found in any significance whatsoever in the present day. Before we can understand why it was a failure, it should be described for what it was: a negation of values held by the older generation. As financial credit and corporations thrived, the call of fresh material opportunities was given to people who were accustomed to making everything on their own, from clothing to beard. It also offered an unprecedented way for the lower class to feel some semblance of the finer things in life. Value was transferred largely from personality to possessions. This value shift was met with rancor that is common with any subsequent generation. Even so, what happened within the course of this particular resistance was uncommonly disquieting. Foreign traditions of Buddhism, nomadic tribalism, and existentialism imbued the movement. Calls for freedom were heralded by Dr. Martin Luther King Jr. who, inspired by Gandhi, rallied non-violently but passionately against the horrors of segregation and racism. Racism was mainstream, built into the American Constitution to discriminate against minorities and women systematically. What Dr. King accomplished with the Civil Rights Movement informed the counter-cultural movement.

Concurrently, other methods for consciousness expansion were showing promise to quell ignorance and other problems facing humankind: the advent of psychedelic drugs.

Drugs have been a factor throughout human history, but it was not until they were implemented scientifically in the 1960s that their true potential was first unveiled.

They then became the most convenient form of potential consciousness expansion, most informal metaprogramming. When drugs became a forbidden activity, suddenly respected and prolific university professors were criminals.

If Dr. King sparked the ideals of the transformations attempted in the 1960s, Timothy Leary sustained them for as long as he could. There is no doubt that Timothy Leary was an unconventional character in academia, but his morals, motives, and missions were all reasonable. Timothy Leary desired what Nietzsche had desired in his time— to bring all persons away from suffering and into the realm of metaprogramming where equality was both a right and a practice. In other words, he wanted what Dr. King wanted, but using different methods. Timothy Leary was less misunderstood than Nietzsche because the hegemony does not desire, as it turns out, to have a society of metaprogrammers.

As for the validity of the War on Drugs, it should be pointed out that the attempt to move to a higher state of consciousness is risky, and while certain drugs are a possible option, they are not the sole path.

The War on Drugs has been proven to have its origin not as an outcry for our nation to be rid of drugs but rumored to be a way for Richard Nixon to isolate and vilify his enemies all while making them the nation's enemies. Nixon was in opposition to counterculture and the already oppressed black community. One of Nixon's advisor's John Ehrlichman confessed as much in an interview with Harper's Magazine. These groups were undermining his agenda, so Nixon moved to associate the black underclass with heroin and marijuana with the hippies. By then declaring these drugs illegal, the groups were able to be targeted.

So people who desired to experience the purported benefits of these psychedelics were now criminals— enemies of the state to be carted off in already cramped prisons along with murderers, pedophiles, rapists, and terrorists.

The War on Drugs is a front that takes citizens and strips them of their civil liberties, their free will to investigate themselves to their satisfaction. There was some credence to aspects of the War on Drugs, to the prohibition of some drugs due to their addictive properties. Heroin, cocaine, and even LSD, are dangerous in the same way that Nietzsche's path was dangerous. If you are not using the tools for consciousness change intentionally and with the wisdom of therapeutic research, the risk of more significant problems is assured.

Regardless, the reason why we must not regard this ban on drugs as moral is both the effect it has on society and ourselves. In today's system, an addict caught with drugs needs punishment, not rehabilitation and treatment. And that is what is so immoral about the War on Drugs. It creates a profit at the expense of addicts, who, too often, are already stricken with poverty.

Interestingly enough, Leary attempted to use specific psychedelics to reduce recidivism rates in criminals. The results of that experiment were not incredible, but I think the fact that it is one of the only legitimate experiments using psychedelics indicates a real issue. Drugs can be a powerful and useful tool for consciousness change. That didn't matter, though. The War on Drugs turned a non-violent matter of freedom into an uncontrollable violent frenzy. Redacted were all the research papers on the cognitive and therapeutic benefits of these substances. And many people who simply desired what Leary and Nietzsche wanted of the world are now victims of the cause for peace.

This is why the counter-cultural movement of the 1960s was also a failure, though it fought hard. A failure in the sense that it did not accomplish the eradication of unnecessary suffering in the world. It did however, make people freer.

In any case, the War on Drugs turned it from a movement to an internalized struggle. And a need in the heart to be spared from the technology to destroy ourselves— which flourished recklessly— hovering just over the mind, like a massive dragon that would appear and raze all of civilization. To admit difficult truths is to exile oneself from the toxic culture. And though it feels right, it can feel even more wrong to be cut off from the herd, no matter what direction they're going in. That was how the counter-culture grew fearful and docile, rightfully so. And the grip of those in power who resist the ideas of equality, metaprogramming, and prosperity solidified their grasp to further their heart-wrenching machinations.

Question: If you knew how to metaprogram, how would your life be different? What goals or dreams would you like to see done? What things holding you back would you opt out of in yourself?

Part Two: The Now

"Now! This is it! Now is the time to choose! Die and be free of pain, or live and fight your sorrow! Now is the time to shape your stories! Your fate is in your hands!"

-Auron, Final Fantasy X

5

"To tear down a factory or to revolt against a government or to avoid repair of a motorcycle because it is a system is to attack effects rather than causes; and as long as the attack is upon effects only, no change is possible. The true system, the real system, is our present construction of systematic thought itself, rationality itself, and if a factory is torn down but the rationality which produced it is left standing, then that rationality will simply produce another factory. If a revolution destroys a systematic government, but the systematic patterns of thought that produced that government are left intact, then those patterns will repeat themselves in the succeeding government. There's so much talk about the system. And so little understanding."

-Robert Pirsig

As you can see, when a wave of individuals seek to bring humanity to the point of becoming metaprogrammers, there is failure. Why is this? Well, there are many people in the world, and as stated earlier, many of them either don't know or can't do anything about their poverty, ignorance, and greed. The disproportion of wealth aside, our evolutionary processing as a whole is still mostly out of our conscious control. Each generation, especially in the past few hundred years, have been trying to advance our plot only to reach maddening, disappointing results.

You may have come to a point now where you may desire to be a metaprogrammer or to help others become metaprogrammers. But the fact remains that this information is not sufficient to satisfy the goal of progress. Even so, some feel there is a tipping point on the horizon with the issue of climate emergency, which begs the question of the best hopes for mankind.

I reiterate the failures of thinkers before me only to point out that I also may have faulty reasoning— those who have failed successfully with the noblest causes in their hearts. Looking out and into the universe, though, my optimism remains. Keep that in mind as we move on to critique the modern world. We shall spend some time analyzing our common impediments to a world of radical consciousness expansion in hopes of finding a way in which to bypass them once and for all.

Today I believe there is something futile about the way activism is working. It creeps in mostly as unsolicited posts on social media or call-out culture. Consumerism is rampage and interfering with any chance for peace of mind. Every problem addressed seems to be solely using production, including, unfortunately, mental illness.

Civil rights and equal rights are still not a given. Not in the United States and especially not globally. Thus we have seen the formation of Politically Correct culture and their devout knights, the Social Justice Warriors. Regardless of your opinion on this kind of activism, it is not going anywhere; it could even continue to develop and become more efficient.

That outrage cultural movement put more emphasis on the need for human rights than our collective unconscious harvest of dwindling resources. Both are dire issues to be sure, but if the hypnosis of the culture remains focused on how unfair things are rather than actionable solutions, then apathy will set in regardless of any meaningful progress. Complacency will soon follow. This new form of activism isn't exactly counter-cultural. It, for the most part, begrudgingly exists alongside it to target specific linguistic choices made in the dens of a toxic culture.

Odd contractions manifest upon speculation. Today, no television show would get away with having a protagonist like Archie Bunker. The way he spoke and the thoughts he had were passable decades ago, but in today's media, anyone who channeled him would be shamed to the point of cancellation. Which, fine, I guess. We devour protagonists like Walter Walt or Rick Sanchez. Mass murder is one thing; they just better not be a racist. It evokes the fallacy of missing the point.

One must learn to speak carefully, lest they incur the wrath of those knights. The worst aspects of PC culture are found in this unfolding of how we speak—each line scanned for any trace of racism or sexism, which immediately nullifies the meaning and message of what the other person is communicating, however important it may or may not be. One can get lost in what's really at stake in shutting a person down for expressing themselves: human rights. Perhaps this preoccupation for language analysis in the PC culture stems from the generation that must have instant gratification.

What comes from this is an emphasis on calling out bad behavior in the way of public shaming rather than an attempted discussion of indiscretions for betterment or healing. Worst of all, there is a priority for wanting to win an argument rather than improving the state of anything. That isn't the true source of what is wrong with PC culture, however.

The fatal flaw seems to be a disconnection between the individual and how all corporations operate. Author Anna Lappé states, "Every time you spend money, you're casting a vote for the kind of world you want." This idea shatters so many myths about the boundless power of corporations. There is a distinct trail of where one's money goes. It is one of the most powerful ways you exercise your political rights as a citizen of this world. Where and what you will your dollar to go to is what you ask to exist.

PC culture would find it meaningless to those who wish to adopt a less consumerist, eco-friendly lifestyle. This is because they believe it's the corporations who are responsible for what ails the world, not the individuals. As studies *have* shown, the corporations are culpable for the majority of carbon emission and pollution, not the individuals in a population. However, individuals in a society choosing what they buy are where corporations get the means to thrive and dominate. The origin of our modern-day corporations and how they came to power are a direct result of human needs and desires being unfulfilled. Hint: This model remains in place, though the onslaught of new products has done nothing, as it turns out, to make us much happier. We need to hold corporations accountable while still acknowledging our roles in where we are today.

For example, if enough people stopped buying single-use plastic, eventually the manufacturers would have a profit loss. They would be *forced* to either stop producing or canvas the consumer to learn what alternative was acceptable. Popular consumer demand would leave them no other option. There is a myriad of companies abusing the planet and have no cause to stop because of profit, but also because of demand. Understand that the climate emergency was willed by former generations who wanted materials for convenience in life without any thought of the consequences. This is why although the recent straw ban seems silly and pointless, it actually sets a remarkable precedent for other products we must proceed to admit are unsustainable. The onus now falls upon *us* to identify what is poison and stop purchasing it.

Even given that, this ideological shift upon Politically Correct culture would also not be sufficient for the progress we seek, because the reality is a lot of people have been put under a habituated loop of fast food, debt, and a need for any kind of pacifying stimulation (all these things at the expense of the health of the person in question). It all circles back to those passive people, far from the threshold of lasting metaprogramming. Those who will, through no fault of their own, be raised in poverty and, in turn, raise their children in the same fashion without any energy for what would be good for the world or the future. Relentlessly tired, they shall exist with bad imprinting, conditioning, and subsequently mental illness.

Let's look at the issue of this idealized world of metaprogrammers from another angle. While there are an enormous amount of people who claim to have the answer to this conundrum, I would like to point to the philosopher Robert Pirsig, who saw this great malaise within modern society as the misguided division between the Classical and Romantic schools of thought. Classical understanding roughly conforms to masculine traits and Romantic to feminine. This is not true as a whole, but culturally speaking, it is. Women demonstrate a favoring of intuition over logic and men vice versa. This is not to say there are not exceptions, this is simply a generalization. In fact, Pirsig desires to say both are vital and must be enabled to coexist. The union of the Classical and Romantic understanding is what Pirsig dubs Quality.

Quality is something Pirsig initially refused to define in his works. See, he thought we had a tendency to leap too quickly to rationality, to labeling things. It missed the point of what a thing truly was. As you can feel what Quality is, especially when comparing the *value* of one thing to another. Just a bit like the Force, really. Or even a modern, sounder incarnation of Plato's Forms. Quality is that feeling of caring, of improvement, of "something better." Art would not exist without Quality. Nor would any innovations except in the most technical or scientific sense.

Instead of an immediate explanation, Pirsig decided to write two books describing Quality. First in its essence, then in its application. His final explanation of Quality after almost a thousand pages on it is settling to calling Quality "good as a noun." This concept of Quality plays seamlessly into the ideals we are discussing as it is supposedly responsible for the development of consciousness and so on. To understand this, Pirsig explains further that there are two types of Quality— Static Quality and Dynamic Quality.

Static Quality is the established pattern of a set of information— how it exists. Our current iteration of DNA is an example of Static Quality. But there is also Dynamic Quality, where within the DNA there are codes for augmentation, evolution— something better is on the way. Quality operates in the universe because it is more moral for it to manifest higher consciousness than to not. Being is more moral than non-being. We must experience a proper balance of Static and Dynamic Quality.

The metaphysical structure of Quality includes a compelling hierarchy not unlike the chart of evolving consciousness from chapter one. At the bottom of

Pirsig's list of everything is the inorganic. From there, it's organic, social, and intellectual.

Here is one of Pirsig's most important thoughts— a diagnosis of the most significant issue we face today:

"We live in an intellectual and technological paradise and a moral and social nightmare because the intellectual level of evolution, in its struggle to become free of the social level, has ignored the social level's rule in keeping the biological level under control."

My assertion is that poverty, oppression, and mental illness ought not to be complex, insurmountable issues that require separate solutions, at least theoretically speaking. In one sentence, I feel Pirsig nailed it. This is because humans have simple and known needs. The time we live in has not changed what our needs are, only our methods of accessing them. Dynamic intellectual ideas are more "moral" than static social structures; thus, the way we are operating as a society is unacceptable given the prowess of our intellectual ideals.

Where do we begin to reconcile this? The truth is, we may have everything we need for the successful undertaking of a world of metaprogrammers.

Question: What are some benefits of PC culture? What social change or good will come from it? Are today's civil rights leaders as effective as they were fifty years ago?

6

"You never change things by fighting the existing reality. To change something, build a new model that makes the existing model obsolete."

-Buckminster Fuller

Architect Michael Reynolds is a ragtag survivor of counter-culture movement of the 1960s. That is, he is a man bent on changing the consciousness of mankind, and he is actively doing so at the time of this writing. Having gone through the traditional path of becoming an architect, Reynolds was disgusted by the opulence and decadence of Western culture. It was this reaction that led him to devote his life to radically sustainable habitats through the creation of Earthships, which he believes have the potential to abolish poverty and, as a bonus, severely diminish waste and pollution. Tall order, right?

There are many thinkers whose works for betterment entail philosophy, theory, or entertainment. But Reynolds is a thinker who was able to apply his thoughts into pragmatic solutions. In an isolated section of Taos, New Mexico along the Rio Grande there is a real life Rivendell. A sequestered place of magic where people design living spaces that exist in tandem with the natural world. It has been nearly fifty years since Reynolds first began developing these experimental structures, and they have come to offer these six things in one design:

1. Building with natural and recycled materials
2. Thermal and solar energy for passive heating and cooling
3. Solar and wind electricity
4. Built-in food production
5. Contained sewage treatment
6. Water Harvesting

Though these six principles are all things the Earth *freely provides*, and we are presently very capable of harnessing, there are places in the world where people are being deprived some of these things. In Flint, what's missing is clean water. Relying on the government, citizens have been completely shut down and crippled for years. Without clean water and energy, a community or city cannot thrive. It can barely survive. The people of Flint became victims of a municipality. Providing clean water ought to be an unconditional requirement of any ruling body. Or, at the very least, help people in setting up water harvesting stations. This is but one example of how we are failing the world at large when in some sense, it's within our control.

People are either unsure or unable to learn how to become self-sufficient. People still pay their electric bills when an alternative exists, one which would ultimately benefit them, but we can once more see this conversion can't or won't take place on a meaningful level. Reynolds wishes to spread the design and usage of Earthships as far and wide as possible. Although there are some drawbacks, the magnificent axioms that follow are logically sound:

1. You can live in a safe home made from what other people are carelessly throwing away.

2. Housing can be created with function rather than form in mind, meaning you can design a house that can heat and cool itself. This is sacrificing vanity or how something ought to look in exchange for how it ought to operate.

3. Corporations have set a monopoly infrastructure to power cities at the expense of the planet. Every month you pay for electricity you are choosing to contribute to any potential damage. The truth is you can generate your own electricity and not be trapped by electro-maniacal companies who discourage or attempt to suppress alternatives.

4. What you eat can be grown locally, even on your own land if you have some. This would diminish grocery bills and processed foods by however much you desire. In fact, a more plant-based diet is scientific proven to make you happier, healthier, and less financially strained.

5. Our oceans do not need to be where we put our waste. Innovations have come including self-contained septic tanks that require no manual draining, composting toilets, and even a machine that converts

feces, urine, and gray water into clean drinking water.

6. The rain that falls from the sky can be harvested, filtered and used several times over for showering, drinking, watering your crops, and toilet water as opposed to water from a grid that is used once and then wasted (and sometimes contains heavy metals). This would eliminate the need for a water bill. Most every location and climate on this planet provides enough rain to meet a family's needs.

Earlier I mentioned drawbacks. Earthships require a shift in consciousness counter-cultural in nature. If that sounds frightening, it should; we know that movement was an overall failure. One must examine every aspect of what they've experienced so far in terms of living spaces. It is true that things are lost in the conversion. Earthships cannot look however you want them to look. It requires a lot of upfront costs. Even the most advanced and recent models are experimental in nature. There is a philosophy that must be adopted before considering or accepting Reynolds's solution because, though he certainly is addressing six vital needs, they are also ones the majority of society would most likely refuse. As Reynolds put it, "The Earth became a sacred place that I wanted human life to embrace rather than exploit." The current way we build housing and pollute our planet is going to have severe consequences. But that doesn't have to be the case.

Another problem with the ideals of building zero carbon homes is the government and certain industries will end up losing out. It's why they've lobbied and conditioned people to become so dependent upon their services so that any attempts to get out will result in extreme frustration on the part of the individual and their peers or family. Reynolds, in fact, was caught up in an intense legal battle back when he first started building Earthships. His designs didn't conform to the permits and building codes of New Mexico. It was a worthwhile struggle because it also meant the promise of an autonomous, comfortable living space which didn't rely on the grid for anything.

On the other side of the argument, those in power cited the buildings were unsafe. This is comical when one considers the toll our traditional methods are having on the planet. So Reynolds was eventually able to establish his "Greater World Earthship Community," a vast plot of land that serves as a sustainable housing test site where normal permits and law are eschewed in favor of finding new, experimental living spaces. It is a pocket of freedom, and it is our task to find other pockets of freedom in this world to better facilitate freedom within us and cultivate metaprogramming practices for life.

Even more detrimental than government barriers, some people won't ever want to give up their materialistic, extravagant ways. Many are so ingrained in those ways that even the mention of vegetarianism or minimalism is an insult to them. For now, I would just like to say what Michael Reynolds is attempting is the kind of consciousness shift we ought to at least consider. He is a person whose idea could save an otherwise doomed cycle of birth, reproduction, and poverty. Getting and staying debt-free is a nice starter pack into the Michael Reynolds philosophy. I'd like to think it's as simple as wanting fewer things.

So perhaps it is not specifically Earthships themselves that must be taken away from this chapter, but their principles. Earthships are just a comprehensive storehouse of things I'm saying people need. On top of that, I've personally experienced Earthships. I've lived in them and know they work very well (I went to where they were first created as a skeptical volunteer). I've lodged in several different ones in the dead of a Taos winter and can tell you they need no secondary heating source. There was kale and other vegetables growing inside of them. In fact, it was necessary to open a vent on the roof during those December days so the plants wouldn't overheat. I think any usage of the Earthship principles I've laid out are beneficial. Earthships aren't the only housing option or solution, but they certainly seem to address more concerns than others.

Realistically not everyone will adopt options such as Earthships. But if everyone leaned into some of these principles, happiness, self-sufficiency, and personal power would be framed in an entirely different way. As Ryder Carroll put it, "We live in a commoditized culture that convinces us that our solutions must be acquired, that something or someone will finally make us whole. Our search takes us ever farther away from ourselves. Though we can greatly benefit by keeping our minds and hearts open, we remain our own responsibility." Focus on what you *need*.

Question: How important is it to you to not have to pay a utility bill? Would that be a greater motivator for you than a healthier planet? What are some objections you can think of living off-the-grid?

7

"Heterosexuality is not normal, it's just common."

-Dorothy Parker

Whether or not Earthships or some solution like it ever adopt a greater following, you must concede Reynolds is addressing six base human survival needs that, if bestowed, *would* challenge poverty. Other obstacles that impede consciousness expansion are greed and ignorance. These are often inextricably linked to poverty.

As these issues arise from our current social and consumer practices, it is vital that we challenge the notion of families, those modern tribes imprinting feeble programs onto an unsuspecting generation. The truth is some people should not have children. Yet it often appears they are the ones who do. People who ultimately become victims of a system that teaches sex in the most ambiguous way possible. Rife with contradictions, abstinence-only education is perhaps worse than no sex education at all.

That's why it's sort of funny that a population of non-reproductive individuals is so often attacked. Some of the most common causes for PC culture to champion are homosexual and transgender identities. As they are in the minority, they are oppressed and hated. However, the artificial familial units these people produce are essential to society. Being transgender is a very dangerous proposition now, but in the coming years and generations, it *will* be heralded as brave for providing groundbreaking developments in gender and social studies. These people are changing our antiquated view of gender, and it's about time.

Toxic masculinity is often cited harshly by PC culture and that is entirely valid, but there is also toxic femininity, which also nurtures fallacious gender roles and expectations. Some parents would rather vomit what they heard from their parents before allowing their offspring to develop the ability to think for themselves. It creates a slew of societal pressure disorders and reinforced dogmas that are nothing but dangerous.

The default function of a cis-gender female should not be *mother.* Certainly, there is the biological imperative, but all too often, daughters are reared and then ridiculed for not having children. So they acquiesce under pressure simply to appease the external world, and ultimately become unhappy parents themselves. This is an example of toxic femininity— the association of women being homemakers. Though that tradition is being challenged, its effects remain apparent. The aim is to declare that gender roles shall no longer be so stringently applied. Instead, let's stringently apply sex positive education that includes the ideas of gender fluidity, healthy relationships, and birth control.

As mentioned earlier, all people should have an appreciation and utilization for both the Romantic and

Classical mindsets, not abandon either under the impression that one is for boys and the other is for girls. The thought patterns and institutions keeping gender roles exclusive can be identified under the phrase *toxic culture.*

Labeling something that is inherently toxic then dividing up into "masculine" or "feminine" disguises the true culprit, and that is the source of this toxicity, the ego itself. The ego is neuter... it manifests through all manner of life and must be challenged from the inside, within each individual.

This is where I really would like to challenge any religious objections to what has been laid out thus far. Many politicians use their religions to inform their moral responsibilities, and somehow, that leads to oppressing the people they are supposed to be representing.

Okay, so you can be religious, but if you ever use that as a reason why you hurt or violated someone's freedom, then that's not being religious. It's just a tradition. A tradition *could be anything,* including a crime against humanity. As the band AJJ so passionately sang, "People are my religion, because I believe in them."

Remember earlier on what Stephen Hawking said— there's a chance that we could have been uncaused, i.e. coming from nothing.

Another thing to note is moral relativism. Where you're born determines what you'll initially believe in. Judeo-Christian ethics drunkenly pilots Western consumption. It doesn't matter that Jesus most likely wasn't white.

Faith would be much cooler if it weren't derived entirely from fear. This hand-me-down litany of unexamined ideals from generations of people who didn't want to accept a "return to nothingness" that is so worth the occasional contemplation. So in summation, don't take your God's wrath out on people. He can do that himself if he's real. Now that that's settled, let's delve a little deeper into being queer.

Queerness is often vilified because of homosexual practices, but technically queerness could be attributed to a heterosexual individual. Queerness is simply abnormal traits in an individual relative to the cultural norm, such as the conscious decision not to have children. Once a damnable secret, queerness is now becoming gradually more and more accepted worldwide. Scientific research suggests homosexuality serves the biological function of population control. These insights were either not explored or had been suppressed, although throughout the animal kingdom, homosexuality happens frequently.

Science was once bound by religion, and that movement away to reach higher ground is still happening. Non-reproducing individuals can theoretically offer support to other offspring in the family. The idea that homosexuality could be some genetic freak accident or anomalous sin is a commonly held view. However, if that were truly the case, evolution would have corrected the aberration long ago.

So as social acceptance increases over time, more of the population will become comfortable identifying with being queer. One interesting thing to note is how sexuality is entirely dependent on culture. The philosopher Michel Foucault went so far as to conclude that the labels of "heterosexual" and "homosexual" were invented in the 19th century, as previously same-sex and sodomy were forbidden acts, at least in the context of the Renaissance. If you were to go even further back to a place such as Ancient Greece, homosexual activity was rampart and a kind of norm. Pederasty was also common— you see, back then, sexual preferences were not a construct of identity politics. They just *were.*

Due to this myopia, queerness today is alienating because politically and socially speaking, there is limited representation and understanding. Politicians are representing heteronormative values, but heteronormative values often negate non-heteronormative values. Despite this, homosexual partners can now be legally married in some parts of the world. Nicely done! But there's still much more work to do.

There is one irksome constitutional issue, one which, until ratification, means another oppressed group are not fully protected against discrimination. It's very aggravating that something as simple as the Equal Rights Amendment still hasn't passed. This legislation would declare that women cannot legally be deemed inferior to men in the United States. Only one more state is required for its passing. It's been nearly a century since it was first drafted and it still has not been added to the Bill of Rights. This is sickening. Historians point to Phyllis Schlafly, a conservative political activist for lobbying against the ERA in the time it was being pushed by woman's liberation groups. Schlafly didn't want equal rights because then women would be subject to the draft and lose other privileges. It turned into a war over maintaining gender roles with Schlafly fighting to essentially maintain women's subordinate status in society. It was a strange thing, but it worked. Thanks to the work of people like Schlafly, though gay marriage is legalized, being a woman *still* is not. The hope is that the trends of late are moving the system into at last accepting the concept of equality.

We seek to depend less on the political process if its function remains to keep people down. The good news is more representation has appeared that at least respects or encourages sex education, queer culture, and feminism. At the same time, instead of waiting for representation, it may be more fruitful to exploit loopholes for freedom— metaprogramming offers a greater degree of freedom to its dedicated wielders but also there are places where this freedom can be externally experienced more than others (one example of many is the Greater World Earthship Community).

Nonetheless, the way should be clear: equality for all sexes, genders, races, and creeds. This is often seen as so blatantly obvious by some people that they consider it a non-issue. Those people have not been negatively affected by inequality.

White privilege is a real thing, and racism is no longer as simple as hating someone based on the color of their skin. The reality is that the effects of structural racism are still threatening the well-being of minorities and will continue to for some time, even if on paper slavery has ended. That means these minorities must be given an audience. In conversations about racism and oppression, they have priority. The same goes for female and queer individuals. Still though, there are cases where the PC attack against white privilege can be abused. I was recently at a party and I heard an anecdote of an elderly Ukrainian woman who immigrated to the United States. Her whole life she witnessed the worst atrocities of the U.S.S.R. and then she was told she was white and therefore part of the problem. This story has no happy ending, as the woman subsequently went "full Trump," embracing the man's ideologies out of fear and confusion. Very few people thought Trump would be elected. I myself could not conceive of it, especially after the way he spoke about women. Yet there were and still are women for Trump. Not even I can explain that.

Many men have a lot of atoning to do in the form of understanding that these shifts are imminent and well deserved. Listen. Empathize. There is still no commercially available birth control for men as there is for women. As actor Bill Murray once said, "It makes more sense to unload a gun than to shoot at a bulletproof vest."

We have to imagine at least some of the recent bites against abortion could be in regard to (aside from religious objections) the fear that a drop in the subsequent population won't produce enough children to one day care for the elderly. This is a ridiculous attempt to take away women's freedom. The proof as to why can be found in the fact that there is virtually no legal penalty for men in terminating a pregnancy in places where the abortion ban is coming up. Although there are equally responsible.

Where women are shamed for their sexuality, men are praised. It has been same with intelligence. The recent advent of the term "fuckboy" presents a uniquely empowering ability for women, who were previously shamed by all sorts like names like *whore*, *slut*, and *harlot*. Now that women can shame men, they do. This isn't exactly equality, but it is a step in the right direction. It is recognizing dishonesty as a shame-worthy trait as opposed to promiscuity. It is one thing of many that is giving woman more sexual agency as of late.

And with that freedom forecasts sexual activity as more and more for the pleasure and bonding for its own sake rather than reproduction. If women are no longer viewed as submissive baby-makers or masturbation machines by toxic masculinity, then the collective consciousness of equality will be properly solidified. The caveat being that we accept, once more, that a woman does not need to produce children to have value in society!

The sincere adoption of this notion would deal a devastating blow to heteronormativity. More men and woman would be concerned with helping the world, not just themselves. Think of the children (that already exist and could use your help if you have the means to support a family)!

For now, the nuclear family is thriving and here to stay, and this book is not attempting to condemn the practice of child-rearing, only to recognize the full implications of it. Some say the decision not to have children is one that might be regretted later in life when someone is too old to bring a child to term, but this too is simply a heteronormative perspective overall.

As for those who have children, may I recommend teaching them E-prime? A few generations worth of E-prime speakers would solve religious warfare pretty effectively. E-prime is a concept derived from the field of general semantics by linguist D. David Bourland Jr., to remove "is" and its verb form "to be" from one's vocabulary. The implications of this are staggering. No longer would there be arguments predicated on who is right.

Instead of:

"My God is the true God."

It would convert to:

"My God, to me, seems the true God based on the latest information I have access to."

Do you see the difference? One is an objective statement, the other is subjective. Encouraging people to do this while they are young will allow them to think critically sooner, and more importantly to be more tolerant to other cultures. It is no secret that the world is gradually breaking down its borders. With the Internet and instant language translation options, people are becoming more and more citizens of the planet as opposed to an arbitrary invisible line where two tribes decided to stop fighting over territory (no doubt because of some disagreement, religious or otherwise). Practice excluding "is" from your language and you might find yourself thinking more clearly and positively.

The War on Terror, like the War on Drugs, was able to demonize one group (Islamic people) and make people believe that they were all terrorists. Even the toddlers in Malaysia were dangerous thanks to the media's fear-mongering. It's the same thing that happens throughout history: they took the example of Charles Manson to show the "evils" of the counter-culture. To justify people's belief that one part represents the whole. This is a fallacy and using E-prime can be helpful in dissolving long held prejudices.

So no more store-bought values and ideals. Away with inherited morality. Question even my message!

Question: In what ways do you consider yourself queer, relative to society at large? Are you ashamed of this aberration? Why or why not? Why are you still using "is" to communicate and describe a world in which your senses in no way could apprehend reality-in-itself?

8

"People really will destroy their dreams and even break their own values to meet their needs."

-Tony Robbins

Aside from the idealization of a new paradigm for sexual culture wherein humanity is reproducing more mindfully, there are also the ideals of human happiness for those alive right now, the fulfillment of who we are. Motivational speaker Tony Robbins says there are six basic human needs. They are very simple to understand, but very powerful, nonetheless.

Robbins states each need corresponds to one another, like the vices and virtue balance of Aristotelian ethics. Each need must be met, but also be in balance with what is next to it. Certainty is established in positive patterns and predictability. Knowing you have enough food, money, etc. Uncertainty is the need to have adventures, being spontaneous, and having the energy to break out of rituals that no longer serve you. Significance is the feeling of self-actualization— that your purpose is being addressed and knowing you matter. Connectivity runs counter to that by saying you also need to know others and feel a sense of togetherness with friends, family, your community, and the world. Contribution is the process of giving unto others. It's why a lot of people make art or desire recognition in their field. Lastly, there is growth, always yearning. The lifelong journey of living with passion should never be ceased, which is why entrepreneurs like Tim Ferriss frown upon traditional retirement.

According to Robbins, if these needs are met, you're good. I believe that makes sense, but I should clarify the path to achieving what Tony Robbins is prescribing is the process of metaprogramming with different words. He also advocates for gratitude, goal setting, and neuro-linguistic programming (of which E-prime could be considered a part of).

Ideally, you should take an hour out of your day to journal, reflect, or goal set. It's referred to by Robbins as the "Hour of Power," a practice to dissolve the expectations of others and culture to focus in on what you want your life to be. Even more ideal would be to begin this practice at the start of each day. Before you worry about what to eat or your cell phone's notifications, replenishing your mind and being intentional will better help you in meeting the needs of yourself and the people around you. When people don't have their needs met, they revert to survival tactics and ego games. The worst aspects of our lower programs of consciousness are then engaged to the detriment of all.

Our experiences become our beliefs, habits, actions, and emotions. Who you were, who you are, and who you want to be are all stories. Stories require imagination, intrigue, and unpredictability. We must forge ahead into the higher programs of consciousness and soon we will learn how.

Tony's spent his life drawing upon information that gets people to live the life they want. Our language, movements, and focus are all within our control. Robbins insists that if we don't leverage these three things in an intentional way, our lives will fly right past us.

The way we use our language summons the scope of what we can experience. Self-talk in the throes of anxiety self-impose limits that stem from conditioning. On the other hand, self-talk can be modified to quell anxiety. More on this later.

Posture and movement also greatly inform our mood, but because people are so often at a desk, they literally forget to play. Don't let that be you. It's as easy as getting up!

Many focus on trivial things because they don't see how they can control the bigger things in life. The subconscious mind does not distinguish between past, present, or future. If we allow it to, both painful memories and undesirable futures can engulf us and distort what options are available to us in the moment. The will must be enacted!

And, as we know, much of the world is in a kind of trance for survival. Imprints and conditioning become our beliefs, regardless of how valid they actually are.

In every sentence uttered, there is what is said and the meaning behind it. Lying is a deed that is generally performed by an unhealthy or a mentally skewed individual. The reasons for lying might not even be that they don't want the truth to be known. Sometimes people want that perverse rush they get when lying, and that's empowerment for the wrong reason. Suffice it to say that those who do not engage in or are aware of any metaprogramming activities have programming within that lie to prevent them from meeting their human needs.

Though there are other kinds of lying that all people participate in to net the greatest good, lying is evidence of an unresolved issue within the self. As disillusioning as that may seem, the source of your lie is good to know because it can be investigated and remedied moving forward. A chance to meet your needs and help others: growth.

That might be the most important need, especially because so many people abandon the idea of growth at some point in their lives to stay within their single personality or state (the "greatest hits" of the first four programs).

Now that you've seen what a person *needs* to live, as well as some ways of achieving them, perhaps things seem easier now and the term metaprogramming is better understood. Think of it this way. The problems you're facing now could be solved and then return tomorrow. By identifying them and addressing them at the source, healing can begin. There need be no frustrating mystery about life when we take ourselves to this point. Re-imprinting, *programming*. It's precisely what people go to a therapist for. Metaprogramming is what people who recognize what a therapist does is point to the work that needs to be done then becoming proactive. It's all about getting better, for keeps. Or as Timothy Leary put it, "You can't do good until you feel good."

Question: What are your go-to sources to fulfill your six human needs? Do those sources truly serve you? Or could you find what you need in healthier, more sustainable ways?

9

"Just think of happy thoughts and you'll fly!"

-Peter Pan

Happiness. For those who will never read this book, what can be done for them? We have seen that, while metaprogramming is encouraged as a logical consequence to future people for the sake of survival and more, the present scenario of humankind seems steeped in their less than ideal conditioning with no escape.

Thus we behold happiness's nemesis— sadness. Lifelong wounds bleeding all over years of Facebook timelines are so prevalent. Humor is a coping mechanism for what ails us, but it is never enough to be a lasting solution. There has been a recent glorification of mental illness, and so we must now consider that another symptom of a toxic culture. Part of it would appear to be as a way to bond with others: "You have debilitating anxiety? Me too!" Speaking up about what's bothering us is very important, because mental illness has a harsh stigma surrounding it. However, this very outspoken method to bond with others obviously isn't working. We must accept what is wrong with us and do everything in our power, sometimes on our own, to resolve or manage it. Yes, mental illness can manifest into severe apathy that effectively cuts off one's ability to act. But where does this apathy first come from? I think that is an important question because it may help to shed some light on things.

As you can imagine, I believe aspects of these conflicts have come from external sources— toxic culture. In this book we are striving to run counter to some traditional rules and expectations. The good news is, opposing the culture of today's society generally doesn't lead to executions and outcries of heresy as they once did.

To see yourself in terms of a complex being operating magnificently with the Eight-program model, you see you're here. The mental illness that negates that can sometimes be more powerful. It's a turning inward that's called for, and today we have a tendency to dissolve our entire worldview onto a single screen.

This perpetual digital fugue— it's not healthy. There are scientific reasons why Facebook is addictive and mentally degenerating people's visions of reality, but people are also making valid connections and careers from this new platform. Being aware of how this filtered reality is affecting your health may offer you a chance to muster the energy to combat it.

There is one perspective I would like to offer instead of rehashing what we already know about technology's effect on people and culture. That is the way new devices are less and less understood by the general population. I think the more people own something like a cell phone the less they understand the technical details of how they are able to operate. It's shocking how we numbly reap the benefits of past discoveries and tragic abusive labor and for the most part do nothing to pay it forward.

With the proper sanctions we can achieve discipline, and through that we may find easier access to happiness. Do you really think the likes of Faraday, Edison, Tesla, and Maxwell envisioned the use of their discoveries in electricity and magnetic to be used for such purposes— to unconsciously drain of mental reserves and wellness? To see their innovations languish and robotize a population in constant need of external stimulus because their lives are out of control? If this trend continues, one might be concerned, as more new technology rolls out, less people will understand it, and the gulf of disconnection will unfold further. Under this view, the human needs would be harder to achieve, obscured in a muddle of technology, coupled with mammals trying to escape into a virtual reality paradise they could never truly attain.

When I think of how cell phones have become a digital Swiss-army knife, I have flashbacks to both house phones and flip phones that had buttons on them. What is interesting to me is I never felt buttons were obsolete. And yet one day some trendy brand came up with touch screen technology and it replaced buttons: jacking up the price of what a phone was so you can spend more of your life on it. As phones became more than phones, some held on tight to the old ways in a bout against consumerism. Smartphones are also more fragile. Better phones may have enriched us, and they have also left feeling lonely in new ways.

Modern life urges the sedentary and unconscious passing of time. It runs counter to the mammals we still very much are and nature misses us. But we miss it as well and so the barrier to real happiness could be seen in that sense.

Due to all of this, most people are operating under the assumption that they have some form of insurmountable depression. Depression is actually a remarkably misunderstood subject, perhaps because it is so unbearable and draining to contemplate, especially if it is currently threatening you. Really, depression is an umbrella term describing several different diseases, but to investigate it under the Eight-program model might help to see it in a more advantageous way.

It used to be thought that depression was a matter of fluctuating serotonin levels based on genetics. Serotonin is a neurotransmitter commonly attributed to feelings of well-being, but also has some relation to rewards, cognition, and learning. The truth is that is a far too reductionist view of the issue at hand. Still, it was a wonderful starting point. Our memories, thoughts, and emotions are housed within neurons.

Toxic culture has programmed people to be materialist and to compete with others monetarily. This fixation of material phenomenon has long plagued man and civilization alike, and yet today, we are so deep into that quest of more that we forget the failures of amassing goods and the relationship it has to our mental state.

The epidemic of mental illness also ought to be viewed from the perspective of the human needs. As opposed to what seems to be the most popular route of late: a little pill to take for each issue.

The pharmaceutical industry is a profit-driven entity who, in recent decades, gained the ability to sell direct to consumers in the form of advertising. Prescription pills, for the most part, do not address the cause of an illness, only the symptoms. As they manufacture products to augment lifestyle, truly it is the corporations that get healthier, not those seeking medical treatment for their afflictions.

Another overlooked aspect of depression is nutrition deficiency. Our bodies require food, sleep, and exercise. It is one thing for a person's depression to be so crippling that they are not able to practice those three things, however the ideas of the toxic culture strike again, coinciding once more to seeking the human needs. The fact is that for every person who is legitimately unable to function due to their given illness, there are many more who simply choose not to take proper care of themselves. And this isn't a case of unbreakable conditioning; it's a decision they're making every day.

There is a noticeable link between the War on Drugs and the advent of big pharmacy advertising. Adderall and meth are chemically similar. Yet their societal connotations vastly differ. Prescription drugs often have side effects to create a built-in audience up-sell. Taking something with a side effect of low-sex drive? There must be a pill for that, manufactured by the same people. Our mental and physical health are too important to be exclusively managed in this way.

In the United States, there is an unbelievable statistic. According to a UN World Drug Report, although we are five percent of the population, we consume seventy-five percent of the world's prescription drugs. We also happen to consume way more cocaine than any other country and also lead developed nations in drug overdose deaths.

It is obvious that something is terribly wrong. What can be done about it? Effective change is going to be a long time coming, considering all the profits. But if you want to seek alternative means of feeling better, acknowledge the follies of this toxic culture that both provides and compounds mental illness.

What constitutes an illegal drug and one obtained via prescription is completely silly and arbitrary. LSD can do some serious damage if it is abused. Same goes for cough medicine and sugar. Any substance in excess will kill you. Apples, water— have enough of anything and you could die.

The most extreme derivative and designer drugs, such as crack cocaine and heroin, provide highs or states of consciousness that can be obtained in safer ways; therefore, it is a sound proposition that these two remain illegal. There is absolutely no need to have something so processed and potent taken into your body. On top of that, seeking those kinds of highs bring various risks as they can only be obtained illicitly.

The worst-case scenario is addiction to these substances, as that is perhaps the furthest one could be from intentionally designing a life to meet one's needs.

The point to be made is some things are less deadly than others, and the intentional usage of objects in the world is indicative of a metaprogrammed individual activating their higher programs of consciousness.

I don't believe happiness can be learned. I believe being happier can be. Before we move on, though, consider some of the obstacles you perceive to be in your way, or the patterns you find yourself repeating that consistently prevent you from living the life you want.

Listen up. People with much greater resistance and obstacles than you throughout history often found a way to get to where they believed they needed to be. Some people find the nerve, and others don't.

Maybe you're someone who's been through war or traumatizing abuse. Perhaps your experiences are something you hesitate to even think about today. And it's not about whose pain is the deepest or whose childhood was the worst. Scarring experiences of any magnitude are understandable… but also acknowledge what extraordinary things people are capable of when the proper purpose and motivation is harnessed.

No one gets a pass from trying to overcome what circumstances they've been through, and there are hard-truth solutions to every problem. The point is the human mind doesn't need drugs in most cases. They've just become a common and simple solution to suppress a symptom of a greater issue. And you do have what it takes to overcome what life has or is going to throw at you.

There are all sorts of anecdotes on the pure magic of optimism, confidence, and motivation. Think back to a time when you were so happy that you accomplished something incredible you might not have otherwise. Another barrier to happiness lies in the fact that other people try to tell us what will make us happy. A lot of times, people equate pleasure with happiness if only on a subconscious level. And for the most part, that in turn conditions us to desire something we don't necessarily want! We were taught to want certain things on the basis that they could provide pleasure, and we can likewise be taught to want better things for ourselves. We seek pleasure and avoid pain, but it's so much more nuanced than that. That which is pleasurable now can be painful in the long run, and vice versa.

The way this so often goes wrong is our disconnection to ourselves. We regard our future selves as celebrities or gods, but we hardly take the time to cultivate any of our success to arrive there.

Optimal nutrition is also a proven weapon against depression, Physician Dr. Michael Greger is insistent from surveying the body of medical research that humans function best on a plant-based diet. Too many people are flat-out ignoring what he has to say. A plant-based diet is the only diet that has been demonstrated through scientific evidence, not only to prevent but also to reverse some of the most common terminal illnesses. Some of the most statistically common ways to die are cancer, heart disease, liver failure, dementia, and depression. All have been shown in clinical trials to be diminished in individuals with the adoption of a plant-based diet.

Now, some vegan advocates and activisms are so outspoken and ignorant that people's common association to veganism is the source of constant scrutiny and ridicule. In this age, the reasons to resist a plant-based diet are running out. It does not mean giving up the essence of meat or pizza, oddly enough, as there are wonderful and nutritious analogs to these foods. Even a small effort or change toward a plant-based diet helps. It obviously isn't an easy choice; it involves commitment and habit upheaval. Still, it's worth the effort. And it can bring a new source of joy and healing for your mind and body as well.

Going on a plant-based diet does not necessarily mean I'm sacrificing all the things I used to love to eat. The truth is, when I eat chicken, it's not the meat-in-itself I love the taste of. It's really the flavor, the seasoning, the nostalgia. Those who object most likely suffer from a diet so high in processed sugars and sodium that, over time, their taste buds must receive their fill of those things, or else.

You see, when you lean more into whole foods, your body's sense of taste goes through an uncomfortable whirling. A withdrawal! Cheese is as addictive as some heavy drugs. As the withdrawal passes, one appreciates the flavor of food more. What is the point here? Well, the ingredients of chicken parmesan can be vegan, but the appreciation for vegan chicken parmesan won't be gained immediately. The body must gradually adapt. The takeaway, though, is insatiable meat-eaters don't theoretically have to miss out on anything but the well-documented lethal side effects of a Western diet.

After all, what we should object to is not meat. It is unsustainable farming practices, preventable illnesses that stem from an unhealthy diet, and the idea that depression should be managed as opposed to cured. Appeals to veganism have gone so wrong. Don't even get me started on the consequences of excessive avocado farming. Point is, although it would be nice if tomorrow people stopped purchasing unethical animal products, it won't be happening. That doesn't mean you can't look into the facts behind this issue. What is eaten has one of the most significant roles on you of all.

The debates on what is best for us to eat will not cease for some time, but one thing inarguable is modern society has disconnected us from nature, with its cities and its screen. Man has flocked to cities in hopes of a higher social status— financial gain at the cost of spiritual insight. It is imperative we never forget that only the more recently developed aspects of our brains are what house humanity. The rest of us is animal in the most literal sense. The disconnection is real, and it hurts everything involved. An example of this disconnection would be to ask yourself: when was the last time you went walking around barefoot in the soil? Ever since we ceased with the knuckle-dragging, humankind has been connecting to the planet via the use of our feet. Now we have shoes. They certainly do come in handy, there is no questioning that. But the combination of staying away from nature and being disconnected from the Earth illustrates my point. The cure to society's woes will not come from walking around in the grass but the acknowledgment of this disconnection.

In a neurological and psychological sense we are still a long way from finding a legitimate, empirically tested cure for depression that works across the board. But seriously consider this question before moving on. How many people would still suffer from mental illness if their human needs were being met?

Question: If you object to a plant-based diet on the ground that it does not provide a body with adequate nutrition, can you remember where you heard that from? Was it an actual fact or a convenient thing that justified your own eating habits from a person who already possessed your same conditioning and biases?

10

"The closer you are to someone, the more they blur."

-Ritsuko Akagi, Neon Genesis Evangelion

Now that we have discussed the ills of society's hypnosis, happiness, and accounted for the human needs, there is one other matter I'm afraid is going to complicate things quite a bit. That being other people. After all, what good is being an off-the-grid highly exalted legendary metaprogrammed individual without others?

It was previously stated that humanity is currently working from Program Four evolution to Program Five. Program Four regulates social, sexual, and moral matters. It is only in compassion that an active evolution can truly commence. As it currently is, most of the people you've meet or will meet are so ingrained in their given culture that they will actively harm themselves to conform. That is, they cannot see past their own imprinted social, sexual, or moral conditioning. Bigots with a willingness to do harm unto others.

These people are not going anywhere anytime soon so we must learn how to be on the same planet with them. It's important to accept that you're going to interact with facets of toxic culture every day for the rest of your life. I'm not advocating the way to live a perfect life, but for a way to better handle the ills of life. When others bring you negative energy, how do you react? Is it different from how you wished you'd react?

Some might like to confront ignorance. Unfortunately, in most cases, the only outcome of confronting ignorance, especially from an "enlightened" position will only result in the other person feeling as if they need to confront what they consider to be *your* ignorance. These difficulties are reduced if you practice using E-prime more, but that cannot eliminate stupidity in this world. You can react more intelligently to stupidity you come across. Sometimes ignorance comes from those you love the most. Your friends, your family, even those you admire. They do not have a word for the feeling of hearing something disgusting from someone you love.

If you're like me, you might think it wise to keep your thoughts to yourself in hopes of protecting your sanity (as well as respecting the individual who is responsible for said vitriol). Eventually, there will always come a time where you know you have to speak up. When it comes, accept that sometimes you're going to be proven wrong. Also know there can be a difference in how disagreements with others have gone before. As you begin to apply the principles and practices of these words to your own life, you might find people begin to treat you differently, and then your dynamic with others could change. This is because you are deliberately bettering yourself and they might not be. They might not like their life, but they might be too complacent about it to ever really do anything about it. All things change, but not all change is progressive. And the people you want in your life aren't necessarily the people you have in your life.

When you stand for something controversial, it will put you at odds with others, including those you love. The danger lies in over-identifying with your beliefs at the expense of the people you truly want in your life. Scrutinizing yourself with these methods and utilizing them will eventually lead you to the horrifying conclusion that someone very close to you is toxic culture personified: and nothing you could ever do will aid them in their journey. It is your decision if you choose to continue having that person in your life. I know of many situations where people reach a breaking point and cut someone out. Without compassion toward others we cannot hope to develop past the lower programs, as imposing our will against them, even when we feel right may perhaps brings even more harm into the world.

The idea is to identify what qualities you value most and give your time and energy seeking out and watering relationships you truly value once you've found them. Even just making the effort of having better people around will enrich and advance your motives, and those qualities most will rub off on you. Often you find these qualities in groups or gatherings, where a social circle based on a common interest or mission is already established.

Conversely, if there are people in your life who you find are limiting you or manifesting toxic culture within yourself, it is okay and to decide that you won't be at their disposal. Interpersonal relationships can be so severe as to create trauma, but here's the thing: when someone continues hurting you and you keep them around because of some perceived obligation or desire to resolve a conflict once and for all, you are never going to heal from that pain. All conflicts have resolutions, but that does not mean all your conflicts will be resolved. Some of them will have no resolution, and though walking away never having the answers of how you could have fixed things is an honest tragedy, it doesn't doesn't change the fact that life isn't a movie. Many of your plots will end in cliffhangers. You will never know what's in the other person head, so if you see that all they're doing is hurting you and you do nothing about it, then you're culpable in allowing that pain to continue. Unconsciously or not, you are. And is the pain worth the love? What a question. The way I see it, the love should be worth some of the pain, but the pain should *never* dominate the love. So if you want healing and get to dawning realization that you and this other person cannot reconcile your differences, I often recommend a strict communications blackout from them to develop a deep therapeutic examination of what exactly was so unmovable about the interactions. Often these insights can only come from distance.

Part of life is the acceptance that people leave. It's

the crux of many tales, such as *Casablanca* or *Final Fantasy X*. People grow, separate, and die. All relationships are unstable, impermanent, and therefore all the more precious. Burners like to use the term "radical inclusion," to better welcome stranger and even foes to share in the same space, insisting that people are not disposable. It should be noted that people aren't disposable, that is true, but the fact is they are replaceable. This may seem heartless at first, but what I mean is what you really wish to receive from others is your human needs (if you're really doing things properly you're also seeking to reciprocate that to people). So we find people who embody the qualities we admire and give them the gift of our focus. If it happens that someone (and they will) must step out of your life, I think it's silly to suppose something is gone forever. What you were getting from that person was the feeling of your needs being met, and that can be found elsewhere, I assure you. I seriously doubt any one person is so unique in that regard. Find someone who gives you all the pros and very little of the cons from that relationship. It's simultaneously ugly and liberating: people will come and go, but the wealth and depth of love never has to go with them. It's one of the most challenging hurdles in this life to lose someone regardless of the reason, but please remember things do not necessarily have to become worse as a result.

There is an idiom that I have taken far too seriously in my life. I'm sure you've heard it before: "You can either be an asset or a liability." Assets maintain and often increase in their value over time when taken care of. Liabilities depreciate and cost you, sometimes in spite of efforts to the contrary. My earnest desire in interactions with others is to find a way I can be an asset to people, but especially if it's someone I know and care for. It seems to be a wonderful, simple rule of thumb: just cultivate win-win situations. If someone does something nice for you, show gratitude in your expressions and actions. Find a way to serve them that is meaningful to them.

One issue I'm always grappling with is the line between vulnerability and liability. When two people first meet, the intimacy of their interactions will be revealed in the proportion between how much one is willing to share relative to the other and vice versa. This is why people are so damn anxious about being vulnerable, they fear "over-sharing." That is, rejection on the basis of being themselves. But anyone who would reject you on that basis is never someone you want to have in your life. It's important to understand within the conventions of toxic culture we have all these protocols of how conversations are meant to go. It's a lot fun when meeting people to see how willing they are to go off script.

This logic applies just as well to other people as to yourself. If someone in my life has come to consider me a liability and I'm made aware of it, I will do what adjustments I can to be more of an asset without sacrificing who I am, but if that isn't sufficient and they still regard me as a liability, then I don't hold it against them for deciding not to have me in their life. In fact, I appreciate their emotional honesty beyond measure and hope they continue cultivating the kinds of relationships they are after which I didn't fit the model of. I take no personal offense though I may feel hurt; I know that each side is simply trying to be their best selves. The gradual strain of dishonesty and non-authenticity that would accompany the alternative is far more uncomfortable in my mind.

After all, we must find a way to work together, and sometimes that means parting ways. The trick is to pull this off without lingering hatred. As any hatred is always indicative of your reaction to someone else, not the person themselves.

Everyone wants the ability to be vulnerable to others, but no one wants to come off as a liability. We want to unveil our hearts and hope they don't get deflated or worse, stepped on. Here's how to attract the kinds of people you want in your life: remember, happiness is dependent on the currency of human needs and it's found in each of your decisions. That's a lot of responsibility, so be sure you know the what and why of them and the people and surroundings you choose.

How this all relates in the larger context of this text is that we must strike a reasonable balance between our own beliefs, the bonds that connect us with others, and their own contrary beliefs. To live unconsciously on behalf of a corporation in a city whose goal is to make money at the expense of nature will lead to sorrow. But to outright abandon the flaws of an establish society and go into the metaphysics of the mind may also be considered similarly troublesome. And it is a balance we all must find within ourselves: for it is not always the center that is most appropriate.

After all, we hope to bring people out of the smog of metropolis and toxic culture. They cannot be forced. It must be appealing and advantageous if at all.

Question: List the fifteen or so of your favorite people, half of the list into people you know personally and half you haven't met but greatly admire. Have you ever asked yourself why these specific people are the ones you value? What qualities do they possess? Are you seeing enough of them? If not, find a way to express to them how important they are to you. Now make a similar list of your least favorite people and ask yourself how you can either be more resilient around them or what steps must be taken to lessen their detrimental impact on your life.

11

"A number of porcupines huddled together for warmth on a cold day in winter; but, as they began to prick one another with their quills, they were obliged to disperse. However the cold drove them together again, when just the same thing happened. At last, after many turns of huddling and dispersing, they discovered that they would be best off by remaining at a little distance from one another. In the same way the need of society drives the human porcupines together, only to be mutually repelled by the many prickly and disagreeable qualities of their nature. The moderate distance which they at last discover to be the only tolerable condition of intercourse, is the code of politeness and fine manners; and those who transgress it are roughly told— in the English phrase— to keep their distance. By this arrangement the mutual need of warmth is only very moderately satisfied; but then people do not get pricked. A man who has some heat in himself prefers to remain outside, where he will neither prick other people nor get pricked himself."

-Arthur Schopenhauer

With the interference of other people there is also the question of a significant other or lover. Where friends and family are where we initially begin in understanding the way the world works, puberty and adulthood force us to answer our biological imperatives to mate in one way or another: whether it be through a Hollywood lenses of what romance must be or through your own critical examination of what true love is. True love is the most subjective thing I can imagine, but I'm sure we could all agree that true philosophy is the greatest expression of our rational capabilities as true love is the greatest expression of our emotional capabilities.

It's the Classical and Romantic schism once more. Using the Eight-program model, we can ascertain that what we loosely consider "true love" was an advent somewhere between Program Two and Program Three (monogamy, marriage, mating for life), while "true philosophy" developed sometime after. This is why most people would rather have sex than receive emotional or intellectual stimulation. The need for it is older, deeper, and much more powerful in our biology than rationality. If emotions can be said to often eclipse a person's needs by prioritizing things that are unimportant, then reason is required to see both needs and emotions are satisfied.

Author Joseph Campbell pinpoints our modern conception of love back to the medieval period, where minstrels and jongleurs first performed narratives of a devoted love. Previously, love was regarded as Eros, which was more about the genitals than the heart. Passion was there, but mates were selected by parents. Individualism kicked in, and ever since then most are able to choose whom they marry. It is interesting to realize the way we view love, just as sexuality, is not what love is but only one manifestation of it in a dynamic historical flux.

For some, the pressure to get married can often be so strong that marriage happens for the wrong reason. And if we choose to look deeper and examine the intertwining history of both love and philosophy, we find some even more disconcerting information.

In antiquity, as rationality was being conjured for the first time as a means of understanding the world through natural phenomenon, most ancient philosophers espoused the importance of asceticism in order to focus on scholarly pursues. This meant abandoning the pleasures of the body for the pleasures of the mind. This asceticism was practiced by both the clergy and philosophers alike. And while it is true that asceticism does lead to the higher programs of consciousness, once again you must understand that there are many paths to reach the higher states (which we will discussed shortly). This meant that there is very little discourse on love for the majority of the history of philosophy (with some exceptions, most notably Plato's *Symposium*). As a consequence, these two truths were separated. I don't believe it was until Schopenhauer that the philosophy of love was put to trial. Just before Schopenhauer dished on love, Hegel laid some foundational information related to the origins of self and other.

The following is a paraphrasing of a Hegelian dialectic meant to explain where self-consciousness first emerged. In a chilling prehistoric narrative, Hegel tells of two people encountering one and other then each immediately striving to overcome the other through violence. Out of this encounter a master and slave are made. It is in this hypothetical interaction which Hegel believes the concepts of the self-reflective consciousness first emerged: for me to have a concept of "myself," then I also need to know something that is not myself, "you." When there is another subject in the world, myself as a subject is threatened, hence the conflict. The conflict cannot end in killing the other, because the initial issue of mastery over the other won't actually be resolved. So when the master dominates the slave, it turns out the slave has more power. This is because the master is dependent upon the slave for his power. Not only that, but the slave achieved self-awareness in his servitude. This story is a bleak depiction of humanity's evolution onto Program Three. Program Three is where "I"-ness emerges, self-consciousness, and verbal language. Before this, we were monkeys.

Others are an inevitable consequence we must encounter. They at once have the potential to threaten and enrich us. Hegel's philosophy was not one of love, but definitely important to get into in order to understand the complexities regarding the philosophy of love.

Now, back to Schopenhauer. He considered love to a very important thing: he tied it to our very survival. To Schopenhauer, the ideals of love, romance, and the sanctity of marriage are all ruses designed by our biology to encourage as much procreation as possible. All these conceptions (and how good sex feels) make it much less difficult for reproduction to take place. Love to Schopenhauer is really just the subconscious realization of how good your babies would look if you slept with someone. This is feasible, considering how the dynamics of a relationship or a marriage can be altered once successful reproduction has taken place: maternal and paternal instincts begin to act in the interest of the child rather than their partner or themselves (a very powerful Program Four imprinting), which we all know can be sufficient grounds for why people separate. Love is forced upon us internally from our biological imperative to breed, and then it is also further distorted by the external world.

Modern conceptions of love work in a synergy with *narrative*. This is true for all concepts and experiences, but it is especially true for love. From the time of Aristophanes, we have been led to believe we are not whole and must seek another half or else we shall wither in some half-life. That some synthesis to complete us is waiting in our soul mate. Never mind if this notion is ridiculous or unproven or harmful, it is prevalent to this day. It took awhile, but Jean-Paul Sartre refuted this by saying the project of love could not be completed.

Sartre practiced a philosophy that worked without ascetic ideals. One didn't need to be a monk or a recluse to engage in the study of philosophy because even in the throes of sexual orgasm, the philosophy of love was not as what had previously been imagined. Love was a valid human situation that everyone experience, and therefore was deserving of true study. Sartre was a great proponent of free will in any situation. He even thought prisoners had some internal freedoms. Freedom, freedom, freedom. Phew, that's a lot of freedom. Oh no, too much! Here's a mitigation: with the freedom of the self we allow for the freedom of others.

According to Sartre, when two people look at each other, they are forming a conception of the other that is not for that other being, but for themselves. These two states of being are not the same even though they are in reference to the same body. They are known as the being-for-itself and the being-for-others. To Sartre, love is the attempt to reconcile this discomfort of being apprehended as "object in the universe" by another subject.

The "project" of a relationship to Sartre then is an individual trying to regain their being as it is imagined by the other. To love someone unconditionally is an act of free will, but that love is being directed not toward the being-for-itself, but the being-for-others. This arrangement is mutual for both parties, especially in the case of exclusive, monogamous partnerships.

This is a special kind of interaction between two people because it transcends the normal identifiers. It can bring a kind of significance. It gives us an exemption from the look and objectifying of others in the world. Even so, this project of love and exemption is extraordinarily problematic, as what Sartre believes we seek from love (freedom from the objectification of others), cannot be accomplished. To be a proper lover is to remain an object for another and vice versa. That and all relationships are unstable. If the freedom from others can be taken away on a whim by a partner's departure, then it was never freedom at all. His philosophy of existentialism was one I believe he lived to the fullest.

If you are having any difficulty in understanding why Sartre believes "hell is other people" and the full implications of his problems with love, I recommend you experience his play, *No Exit*. *No Exit* is the scariest piece of fiction I've ever experienced. And it's not even *in* the horror genre. If anything it's more *philosophical* horror. Basically, the story plays out after a journalist was executed and sent to hell. He is taken to what looks like a waiting room. Soon after, two women who have also just died join him and they are locked in.

It doesn't take long to realize that instead of the conventional fire and brimstone torture of hell they'd been expecting from the Judeo-Christian narratives, it seems each one of three is meant to torture one and other just by being stuck in that room together. At first, they insist they won't play into that game, but it isn't that simple. Even the slightest hint of being there becomes an irritation. The three can no longer be without the others: those who are not them, who have formed an image of them that cannot be controlled or returned for purification.

To make matters exponentially worse, one of the women desires the journalist because if she doesn't receive his validation sexually she will shatter psychologically. He also needs her validation that he was not a coward in death, but she can't give it to him, and it is then that he rejects her advances. Meanwhile, the second woman doesn't want the man, but the first woman— but she in turn only wants the man. On and on and on it goes for eternity. None of the three could receive relief from the others, as none of us can truly receive validation of our own being from others.

As a result of his works in fiction and philosophy, Sartre was not only a famous for his thoughts, but also a French celebrity power couple with fellow philosopher Simone De Beauvoir.

Get this: the two massive intelligences collided in college and spent the next fifty years of their lives together. What ended their relationship? Death. That is common enough, a good number of couples celebrate decades-long anniversaries. But Sartre and Beauvoir did not marry. It was a trail-blazing, non-traditional partnership made all the more sensational by their stature at public figures. They did not have children, but they did have other lovers. Sometimes together, sometimes apart. But they always went back to one and other, meeting constantly and writing together. Sartre's view on the philosophy of love was so convincing to him that he refused to live his life as if it were not true.

And so it was, the respect and responsibility of freedom.

I have always marveled at the relationship these two had. Say what you will about them, but there is no doubt they were some of the smartest people to ever walk the Earth. You might imagine that could be in part due to the strength of their bond. One might even go so far as to say it was more intimate and committed than some monogamous relationships. From the outside looking in, it sounds like a wonderful life the two of them shared together. It can't have all been bliss, but what an experiment! It would appear that it was a success for them.

It seems as if the two were confronting the most common objections to love and thus sought to make it as rational as possible. A philosophic love.

A love of wisdom and wisdom of love combined? The Romantic and the Classical collapsing into one all-encompassing system where the division was nonexistent this entire time?

And no matter what nonsense models of traditional or society's metric of love are, part of me believes we shall all desire it and never entirely discount it. The conditioning is too deep, and many will marry. Many more will do so on false pretenses, as Sartre had mentioned. After all, it's much easier to blame your failures on someone else. It seems our greed here stems from the fact that in reality we cannot ever possess anything.

On the opposite end of this existentialist

partnership, there are the heteronormative works of romance, "love at first sight," such as the sitcom *Boy Meets World*. I loved this show growing up. Cory and Topanga's relationship became something I wanted. Two people so committed because of their love. They married after high school. They had children and a happily ever after. How could this not be the case, after all? In that idealized reality, the bonds we form young remain with us for the rest of our lives. I've found this to be so far from the case that it's a bit hard for me to sit in for more than a few episodes of the show, even though I still find it funny and endearing. I think narratives like that have done us more harm than good. They reinforce so many toxic ideas of how people think love ought to work that they hardly prepare one for the harsh realities of romance in the real world.

Yet when we watch these things and compare them to our own experience it can be enlightening. Obviously these are not meant to depict reality, reality must depict itself. It cannot be done through a filter. The value lies in identifying what you think is toxic about the love narratives.

In response to Schopenhauer and other bleak notions of what love truly is, writer Dan Harmon has some worthwhile input: "The knowledge that nothing matters, while accurate, gets you nowhere. The planet is dying, the sun is exploding, the universe is cooling, nothing's gonna matter. The further back you pull, the more truth will endure. But when you zoom in on Earth, when you zoom into a family, when you zoom into a human brain and a childhood and an experience, you see all these things that matter. We have this fleeting chance to participate in an illusion called 'I love my girlfriend, I love my dog.' How is that not better? Knowing the truth, which is that nothing matters, can actually save you in those moments... Once you get through that terrifying threshold of accepting that, then every place is the center of the universe and every moment is the most important moment and everything is the meaning of life."

What you choose to do in life isn't as important as who you choose do it with. Sometimes that means having the courage to do try something alone, but most of the time is means nurturing your relationships. Glass can't cut you if it isn't broken. I've always felt the same way about people.

Thus even in the bleakest of concepts of love, is there perhaps some hope, even if it's in the form of accepting the illusion? Well, if Sartre believed the project of love is self-defeating, what of our own conception of philosophic love? We must doubt its existence at this time due to all the objections leveled against love in this chapter. No, philosophic love is vague and though elusive, not impossible. As humans we err when desire defeats us. We shall continue trying to love in the ways we find most meaningful and fulfilling, even if the present reality is as Schopenhauer and Sartre posit.

Even so, I insist that one consequence of metaprogramming is the beginning of the development for genuine philosophic love: where reason and feeling become one action and we can seek more intentionally just what it is we need. But we have to know what that is first.

With the utter equality of the sexes (an upcoming event I feel must be taken as inevitable) will come a shift in attitudes about sex: sex will be permanently separated from reproduction in our greatest future. And this coincides with our oncoming ascent into the higher programs as a species.

One matter stands in our way before we are able to express the future of this philosophic love, however... first we ought to find out what we can about who are we. For there we shall find the radiating beauty we'll need for the task.

Question: Who was the greatest romantic partner of your life? In what ways did your expectations fall flat in being with them? Did those expectations actually come from you? Were they really yours or did you learn them from an unhelpful theory of love from some sitcom or movie? What lessons have you learned since discovering the folly of Hollywood's portrayals of love?

12

"It is as if we were divided into two parts. On the one hand there is the conscious "I," at once intrigued and baffled, the creature who is caught in the trap. On the other hand there is "me," and "me" is a part of nature — the wayward flesh with all its concurrently beautiful and frustrating limitations. "I" fancies itself as a reasonable fellow, and is forever criticizing "me" for its perversity— for having passions which get "I" into trouble, for being so easily subject to painful and irritating diseases, for having organs that wear out, and for having appetites which can never be satisfied— so designed that if you try to allay them finally and fully in one big "bust," you get sick."

-Alan Watts

This section is an attempt to find out what we truly are. No promises, though. The accessing of the higher programs of consciousness through yoga, tantra, meditation, and psychedelics hopes to overcome the passive patterns of the undisciplined monkey mind, flitting from one fancy to another in order to apprehend something *more*. Specifically, it is said in the philosophy of yoga that within each being is an inner essence which is light, referred to as *puruṣa*.

It is considered folly within this discipline to ascribe too much rationality in understanding this concept of *puruṣa*. Reality is experienced through the senses and channeled further into emotions through the "heart-mind," but beneath all of those things it is hypothesized we are much more than senses and mind. Ego, self, spirit, and soul? From a tantric perspective, *puruṣa* is also said to be linked to all other inner lights, all other beings in every facet of existence. Tantra teaches a strict nonduality, that all things and moments are perfect manifestations of the goddess. It is our dogmas (ego) and language, our grounding in physicality that keeps us from apprehending this *puruṣa*.

So where do we go from here? While it is true that ego is frail and a terrible thing to center your existence around, that very taming of the ego confirms that is it there (specifically in Program Two of consciousness, where it can be found in various stages from depressive self-immolation to megalomania).

The self is not the ego, however. Ego is contained within the self. We are only ever using language (Program Three) to compile a representation of what the self must consist of. Therefore what we often consider to be the self resides in Program Three, though it is not exclusively contained there. It spills out as "I-ness" into the other programs.

We start with the given of brain and body because they are both apprehensible and evident. If our modern conception of self is to go any further, does the yogic concept of *puruṣa* truly offer the pathway to what we truly are? Other teachings indicate yoga without worship and acknowledgment of *puruṣa* is pointless. Still, in a sense yoga can help one begin to know the right questions to ask. If nothing else, we must admit there are things bigger than the ego. And that is exactly what we are preparing to accept together as a species.

Science and religion meet at the concept of light. Science has identified light as discretely energized particles that travel at a fixed speed, a velocity greater than anything else observed. They have also established that there is an unbreakable relationship between matter and energy. As we go on to encompass more than our brain and body into what constitutes a self, we can at least concede that consciousness is a manner of light that is using the neurons of our body to take energy and make it something else. What the implications of this are can't be dealt with much further however. *Puruṣa*, or our soul, would seem to be dependent upon external sources of energy. After all, if the Earth didn't have the adequate elements, our bodies would not exist as they do now, if at all. Consciousness travels through the neurons, as does the idea of *puruṣa.*

Religions principles hold to a tradition of surrender to a higher power. In Judeo-Christian culture, it is the maker God. In the Indian traditions, it is Krishna. Same difference: they are the source of light. Without this surrender, a human is supposedly limited in its potential for consciousness expansion, because otherwise it would not be able to subdue its ego. This is why we must accept at least the possibility of a higher power. A greater energy than ourselves. It is actually an effortless activity when you take into account how weak you are in your little body. Will we achieve the means to transfer out of this fleshy shell? If so, we'll have find *puruṣa* to do so. To find another vessel that could contain it. This will one day become a more pressing issue rather than the thought experiment it is today.

The lower programs of consciousness are Newtonian in nature. That is, they regulate Earthly principles and matters. The last four programs are Einstenian, perhaps preparing us for space migration and more elaborate forms. You see, it is the mastery of the lower programs that support our true ability to experience the higher ones. We are growing less selfish, but that doesn't mean we aren't still selfish. But you see our development for survival and ego was only ever to be able to one day give to others. Our children, our world, our progress. This is another reason why we must be leery of love as it exists today, all too often our love is coming from the lower programs, not our higher selves.

As we at last discuss these higher programs, see that one common theme to all religions is bowing to what is above ourselves. But what is above us is connected to us, rather, there are no divisions. One thing that truly sees all reality, this objective reality we cannot see as humans. That is the religious interpretation. Scientifically, there is no evidence of an absolute objective reality at this time. I can only confirm my brain and body, and even they are but lenses (often cloudy ones at that). The source of all light beckons us further to where the soul is housed within. Meditation is meant to squeegee the mind of the impurities found in our level of reality to get us to a state of oneness... when we get good at this we find ourselves occupying and modifying each our of the eight programs.

Nonetheless, in either interpretation we go with, we are lacking. If we lean into faith we cannot be redeemed by our own self. We require a higher power to accept us before we can ever truly be whole. If that incarnation of a higher power is nonexistent, then whoops! But if scientifically we probe further and further into finding the soul (or as it is more commonly being referred to by Singulatarians: immortality and consciousness transfer) we might spend our lives in thrall to science, a practice that cannot detect a soul due to its metaphysical content (the philosophical and practical specifics of which will be expanded upon in the coming chapters).

We must yield to something, sentient higher power or not, yet still we have to fend for ourselves. Redeem ourselves. Whether I like it or not I am responsible for what I am, what I do, and how I affect others. Not how I was conditioned. Not how any higher power created me. No hypothetical metaphysical light force is required to redeem or elevate the self. But so no elevation of the self becomes too lofty, it must know its place in the universe.

This is what is lacking before we can truly know who we are: we must take the havoc ego brings and melt it down into ourselves.

Beyond normal human consciousness the ego dissolves into something greater than itself. When and if it returns, it does not fear what is above it, but it does deign to be subordinate it to a sense.

In my opinion, this is the tightest tight rope walk a mind can tread. The higher programs are frightening, they reinterpret man as a process run by the universe at large. We have some grasp of why the majority of people have not taken the time to seek within themselves. But now we also can come to suspect that if it doesn't happen soon, we may never have the proper currency to pay our metaphysical light bill.

It is in this step forward we are now able to describe what other states of consciousness people have discovered as well how they got there. It is where our highest hopes for our own future lay: Peace. Liberation. Philosophic love.

Question: Where is your ego? Not somewhere it doesn't belong, I hope. Why don't you find some way to drain your ego's current level, like championing a cause greater than yourself? Find yourself a god that won't punish you for doing the weird stuff behind closed doors.

13

"Sometimes things are beautiful just as they are. Sometimes, trying to manipulate and exploit that beauty will destroy it outright. When people are made to dance, they often lose what made them want to dance in the first place... some things are mysteries... and sometimes those things should remain mysteries. You can't find a frog's life force by dissecting it. Instead, you lose the very thing you were looking for by asking too many questions... at some point, some things should just be left alone, because the next thing you know, the magical subject you were trying so hard to demystify might just walk out in front of a bus. And then you'll never know the forest composed of those mysterious, wonderful trees."

-Johnny B. Truant

In the series *Naruto* there is a riveting debate between the two rogue ninja companions Sasori and Deidira. Deidira's ninja specialty is bombs and he believes art is an explosion: an instantaneous impression that can only exist in the moment when something is first apprehended. After that, the only perception of that piece is hinged upon the memory of that initial explosion. It's otherwise gone.

Sasori on the other hand believes the opposite: that art must last far beyond a moment, it must stand the test of time and still be regarded in order to be recognized for what it truly is. Both argue at length in a most hilarious fashion before a battle against their foes, but I think this debate can be settled by saying both incarnations or views on art could be valid. As you will see, this is just the Romantic and Classical mindset wanting to separate themselves again. The Romantic attitude desires to feel or intuit something, and that is immediacy. The Classical attitude feels things must be examined and turned over before a conclusion could ever be reached.

In my transgressive road novella, *This Never Happened Somewhere*, I took to the task of asking who was better off, monogamous or polyamorous people. But by the time I really got to know the characters, I knew that such a question was far too complex to see a simple answers emerge that would satisfy all parties. Instead, I left it open. Both experiences can be valid, in the same way both kinds of art can be valid with the caveat of having their own specific drawbacks. We have seen Sartre and Beauvoir persisted in their partnership their entire lives, and it is in that deep introspection and customization of a relationship that may be the key to escaping the problems of love.

Earlier it was mentioned equality was still a distant aspiration of our race. What if the project of philosophic love has been damaged by the inequality of the sexes... has that even ever been considered? That's another reason why the relationship of Sartre and

Beauvoir is so fascinating. They were a man and a woman who respected one and other! Beauvoir was not underestimated because she was a woman. Perceptions of being from societal expectations, representations of men and women sully our quest for philosophic love. I think it is even folly to idolize the love these two had, since I've never experienced that directly I can only speculate and form my own conceptions about love that suit me from there.

Whatever we do, we must remember once more that the human race has not completely evolved out of egos and their myriad malfunctions. The solution might be metaprogrammed mating— the invention of philosophic love.

The ideals of romance and child-bearing at first glance seem to dull the edge of philosophical inquiry. You need only to look at some of the most famous intellectuals of all time to see that they were not married (or weren't able to express their sexuality in a healthy manner). The Classical and Romantic mindset are reunited when bliss pulls someone to one side only to demonstrate there was no division after all. All programs of consciousness ought to be sought out because they are available and could make you feel freer than you are now.

Freer to define and seek out your philosophic lover, someone who also prevails in all the programs of consciousness… a new sort of partnership. One that addresses those mammalian and existential objections to love discussed earlier. Our quest for what is beautiful, this becoming of philosophic love is a complex challenge. We ask for beauty without manipulation or power plays out of selfishness.

There is actually some hope in the practice of tantra, which is about way more than stellar sex. Given this, you can almost imagine Sartre's thoughts on love as coming from the perspective of Program Two. That it is the individual ego, insecurity over its territory and where it can exist— being unable to reconcile with the other's "look." If you read over Sartre's work, this is exactly what you'll find. "The look" in Sartre's philosophy is only a problem (albeit a severe one) on certain lower programs.

Tantra seems to be a proto-philosophy to the future *denaturation* of the sexes. Where philosophic beauty is not male or female, but neuter. Union. Here is our chance to troubleshoot the problems we face with "the look."

There are many different forms of tantra, and we have already discussed what is known as nondual Eastern tantra, a discipline that began in ancient India. It involved rituals and initiation by a guru to liberate suffering by means of apprehending the nondual nature of the universe. Over the centuries, its esoteric knowledge spread until Western society seized the word and sexualized it.

In many ways, this was a dick move. It was taking a culture bent on liberation and leveraging it for a better orgasm. But in other ways, it was inevitable that something needed to be done in order to change how we viewed sex. Still, out of respect for tantra as it was originally meant, we shall henceforth refer to any Western tantra as "sex magick."

Sex magick is responsible for many positive things, and it's here I believe we begin to see a historical basis for philosophic love as well as a concrete solution to the objections presented earlier in the discussions of love. Practicing sex magick is the study of bodily intelligence and worship. When it first became proper, another noteworthy event in the history of sexuality had just stuck its landing— the invention of the personal vibrator.

Not long ago, women were often diagnosed with hysteria and given pelvic massages by "professional" doctors. This practice is terrifying to imagine because to be a woman who wanted sex was to be considered hysterical. Due to this lack of knowledge in the ways of female sexuality, the vibrator was invented to spare those doctors hand cramping. Although it has a dubious origin, the vibrator gave women a newfound freedom to explore their bodies and have orgasms in a new way.

So sex magick and the advent of vibrators are, in my mind, the species' movement toward Program Five, where love is not all about sex for reproduction but healing and fostering compassion. The configurations of our atoms are altered in the trance state sex magick may induce.

It is a trigger onto higher programs, and you can imagine is it properly explored with other people (that's why optimized Program Four operation is contingent upon cooperation with others). One commonality between tantra and sex magick is the potential of every moment to be filled with glory. When we engage in the activities of tantra or sex magick, we activate bliss (Program Five). Bliss is neither happiness nor pleasure in the conventional sense. It is the recognition of how nothing in that moment is truly superior to any other moment. That bliss is always possible. The ego is seen as limiting, and our energies are driven from emotion as we transform. Charismatic people are able to tinker with Program Five, depending on their intentions.

The truth is, we need love, no matter how cynical it makes us. I like to think we're all closer than farther from it. Each of us must decide if such a thing is really possible and when it is found.

In the series *Battlestar Galactica*, robots known as Cylons gain self-awareness and revolt against their human creators. They evolve to look human and achieve immorality. In choosing to commit genocide against their creators, the Cylons envy the human ability to reproduce, even though the Cylons already have immorality. They manage, after a period of trial and error, to produce a half-Cylon/ half-human hybrid by having two individuals fall in love. Love, it seems, was what was missing.

In Western culture, love and sex are seen as mutually exclusive. We are able to have sex without love and easily produce a child. Sex magick is the concerted attempt to bring love and sex together. Partners fuse in a way that is set apart from the kind of sex any animal is capable of. We regard the other not as an enemy but truly connected to us. As we exchange our being, limited consciousness is perhaps at last cleared and we breach the boundaries of ourselves with a stimulating, caring touch. It is a power welded in good faith. Harmony is the goal in this erotic potential. Philosophic love is the true graduation in understanding beauty and bliss, brain and body.

Question: List some beautiful things then go look, consensually kiss, and honor them.

14

"The four steps in dealing with an emotion mindfully—recognition, acceptance, investigation, and nonidentification— can also be applied to thoughts. We tend to identify with our bodies. When we're feeling blue and thinking lots of sorrowful thoughts, we say to ourselves, *I am a sad person.* But we if bang our funny bone, we don't usually say to ourselves, *I am a sore elbow.*"

-Sharon Salzberg

A therapist once told me the ills of life could be tackled with either medication or meditation. When I was told that, I imagined meditation to be some mystic art or religious ritual that wouldn't do my skeptical self any good. But what the therapist said is something I now consider to be highly accurate. If the idea of meditation likewise brings the idea of resistance in your mind, perhaps think of it just as a practice of doing something you usually do without thoughts bombarding your mind. What this accomplishes is that if there are negative or controlling thoughts, then meditating can push them into a place not where they can be banished or ignored, but simply observed, accepted, and accounted for.

There is a specific issue meditation seeks to address, but to understand it requires knowing we view the world as it appears, not the world as it is. This is reasonable, as animals perceive the world in different ways because they have different sense faculties. Humans do not have a comprehensive view of the universe through their senses. M-Theory hypothesizes that the universe is actually composed of higher dimensions beyond the three we can see, and even that division is too puerile for the human condition. See, language is incapable of expressing what we might consider the true reality. Language means dividing up reality, but reality is singular. Meditation is the attempt to reconcile this intuition of nonduality with the world we see. We do this so we can come to know it is only being viewed by us through lenses— an attempt to contemplate upon nonduality. It is due to insufficient perception that we have founded language as the closest approximation for our purposes. It is why we have a habit to make divisions rather than unions. Forming a word for something filters what it is. Defining it filters what it is. Then see, each culture subdivides again and again because of their different languages and worldviews.

This specific issue is well-known to yogis or anyone acquainted with Sanskrit. Meditation hopes to rein in *vṛtti-s*. *Vṛtti-s* are the thoughts you hear that come automatically, uncontrolled. Your mind in action. They come in several different forms, but most commonly, they are considered to be unhelpful and detrimental to all long term prosperity and growth. This is because they emerge and seek to be what is most important, although often *vṛtti-s* just lead you to a state of anxiety. It is meditation and the practice of yoga that is meant to still the mind. Not to control our thoughts, but to understand that ourselves are not necessarily these thoughts.

In wondering just what benefit meditation could bring, think once more of the Eight-program model. Yes, the practice of meditation is a confirmed way to access the higher programs. Notice I didn't say mastery. Meditation seemed very tricky to me at first, so much so that I felt like I was doing it incorrectly. Then I felt like it was boring. Like it was work or something. This could be a barrier you're facing. The truth is, this practice is work. Work that must be done one way or another to be the people we need to be. Robert Anton Wilson explained, "The human delusion of being separate from and superior to the rest of the natural order is a kind of narcissistic self-hypnosis. Awakening from that egotistic trance is the major goal of every Oriental system of psychology."

Sensory deprivation tanks (the technology pioneered by John C. Lilly, who also coined the term metaprogramming) are a way to achieve a meditative state by way of inaction.

This is why I believe you can't meditate incorrectly. You can only choose not to meditate. Which, I mean... hell, meditating could be blowing bubbles! I often do bubble blowing meditations. Adults severely underestimate the stress-relieving properties of blowing bubbles. My practice is indistinguishable from any child frolicking with a bubble wand, and that's the whole point! I have one particular thing I like to do. I call it atomic bubbling. Taking one bubble, then bringing it back onto my wand and adding other bubbles to see what kind of structure I can make or how many bubbles I can get to coexist.

Our ancient childhood of wonder may be returned to us now and then if we allow it. And we can still be responsible, functioning members of society.

Meditation could also be thinking about what you learned. It's a personal pursuit that need not attach itself to any higher power than what you're comfortable with. What did you want to accomplish today that would help you meet your needs? This could be something you already do daily. The point is to recognize that, focus on it. Take time everyday for yourself to stop and focus on your breathing. Even if it's just for two minutes. You might find yourself more grounded and more powerful than ever before. This willing and reflective capacity is the most common tool of the metaprogrammer. Meditation is the bridge to the higher programs. The thing that really got me going were the guided meditations on YouTube. The truth is any of them ought to do the trick; you just need to try. Maybe some meditation styles and techniques are superior to others. I used to believe there was something about Transcendental Meditation that was elusively valuable. Nowadays, I see anyone who wants to receive the benefits of meditation can for free. The idea is to start acknowledging and comparing these altered states of consciousness, how they differ from your normal state. Breathing meditations are an excellent starting point. Your very existence is composed of those breaths. Have you ever thought of that? How that motion within allows you to be?

Or ask yourself, if you're an atheist or an agnostic, what is your personal limit barrier to unbridled acceptance to the concept of nonduality?

From now on, try to leverage any type of meditation you find in your journey to facilitate the obtainment of your human needs.

Question: Does the costs of practicing meditation truly outweigh the benefits? If so, why do you think so?

Part Three: The After

"Anywhere can be paradise as long as you have the will to live. After all, you're alive... and you can find the chance to achieve happiness anywhere."

-Yui Ikari, Neon Genesis Evangelion

15

"Myths are like dreams in that without them, we're as good as dead. However... dreams can be dangerous. Anybody living with one they are unable to manifest, articulate and/or share has, perhaps, already begun losing their handle. In the face of unknowns, I appreciate handles. They let me float in the abyss, knowing there is a grip to return to somewhere. Occasionally, I feel the only real handle there is, is my physical body. It's a relief to release that grip on occasion— to collapse, drop my big act and "die."

-Antero Alli

Now that we are armed with the knowledge that there are greater states of consciousness available to us, how they have been veiled from discovery, and how we might transcend those obstacles, what exactly are they? Here are the latter four programs briefly described:

Program Five

Ecstasy: Rapturous fugues or creative bliss, the mind supersedes the body to make art or engage in something so intently the body is temporarily put past itself. Healing is instrumentally linked to this program. Our senses that visualize and conceptualize our experience offer to move into a more internal aesthetic space. The start and recognition of one's self as pleasurable above what is culturally taboo—perceptions based in what feels good rather than what feels right. The extended prolonging of an orgasm is probably the simplest way to experience what this program is. The upper-class of society has long enjoyed the benefits of Program Five because of their ability to live in leisure, but complications arise when one remains here. The sociological explanation seen in why the rich are getting richer and the poor are getting poorer.

Program Six

Mastery: this is known as the metaprogramming circuit. At this level of consciousness, one begins to knowledgeably play with and tweak their less than ideal installed circuitry. To replace them with prettier hoops and loops via reconditioning and re-imprinting. A paradigm shift within the self. At this point in consciousness evolution, an individual operating Program Six truly begins to stand out from the majority of the human population. Monks, geniuses, and the like become so enveloped in these ideals as to negate the social order and cultivate an awakened, anti-robotic state that can be lived in. Psychedelics have only recently brought this program into the mainstream.

Program Seven

Unity: Building off Programs Five and Six, the individual, leveled past common human consciousness, engages with its relation to the world and the universe as a whole and sees itself as one with it all. Nondualist ideologies are fully embraced... the collective is achieved. We fully see and know barriers between all things are an illusion. People who consistently channel this state are considered by the rest of us to be mystic. Most importantly, we understand we are not the center of anything but only a random point. Think the collective conscious from the psychologist Carl Jung. The more this state is reached, the more lasting empathy will be imprinted upon the user. The future state of evolving into this program is far off, but it will involve our species understanding themselves in terms of atoms and molecules, the DNA. We will decode the script and really begin to see all we are to become. This is because there is a code in the DNA that has been present from the very beginning. Our atoms have been in motion with the kind of energies that create the social and the intellectual patterns. Billions of years ago, this sentence *existed*.

Program Eight

Singularity: This is the highest program documented in this consciousness model. Initially, as a skeptic, I didn't like this one much. But after careful consideration, I admit it's a logical possibility. This program predicts some truly incredible things, like out-of-body experiences and even more wacky parallels to the nature of quantum mechanics. In the same way that a sign of an activated Program Seven individual is the adoption of a nondualist reality, Program Eight recognizes even further the bond between all things. As Einstein struggled to explain how two atoms, despite being at the other ends of the universe could pass information back and forth if they've previously interacted, and do so at faster-than-light speeds (quantum entanglement), so too does this program anticipate the same is true for all atoms. That the barriers and distance between all things is another illusion conjured up by our puny human consciousness and, in reality, things are non-local (everywhere and everywhen). After all, if the Big Bang is to be believed, then the distance between objects and everything humans perceive wasn't always a factor to the properties of the universe. As a matter of fact, one could go as far as to doubt some scientific data and measurements taken about certain phenomenon given a) the primitiveness of our instruments and b) the fact that the universe isn't necessarily homogeneous.

There is a fair degree of certainty that the speed of light is both constant and never exceeds 186,000 mi/s. However, not only is light's speed a recent human observation, it has also been measured in the only places we could reach or observe. One wonders then if light speed was always the same. Going even further with this, can this speed limit actually be broken? As preposterous as this may seem, read on to see the implication of apprehending Program Eight and beyond.

On interesting thing to do know now that we have explored the entirely of this model: depending on who you consult, some put the metaprogramming program as Program Seven and the unity program as Program Six. This discrepancy is amusing to me, as the higher programs are so flighty and abstract. Personally, I consider the metaprogramming circuit as having appeared before the unity circuit based on the fact that mastery of metaprogramming is probably conditional to Program Seven unity as a species.

Tapping into these higher programs is something people do now and then. It's the habitual or purposeful attempt to experience these states, which is so very rare. As stated earlier, meditation, yoga, and psychedelics are the most common avenues to get to these latter programs. And I mean intense practice into one of these. Advanced yoga or Ayahuasca.

Our society has successfully outlawed the majority of psychedelics, and the reasons for that are known to be egregious. Understand the value of the Eight-program model and why you're probably only just now hearing of it. It is suppressed information, partly because the man who created it was an enemy of the state at the time. Academia promotes metaprogramming without calling it metaprogramming, so it's time we evangelize this particular model so it may receive the recognition it deserves. The greatest strength it possesses is as though it is a complex psychological concept, everyone can use it if it is explained properly.

There is nothing wrong with occupying the first four programs, but there are newer options and experiences of consciousness that will bring you to a greater understanding of yourself and the world around you. Actually, what's wrong could go wrong on any of the individual programs. It is best to first recondition the negative aspects of your first four programs before intentionally treading further. You can consider many of the higher programs are easily abused. Cannabis is a cheap and simple method to Program Five bliss, but because stoners rely on the drug for the experience they do not separate the two or even wonder how else to achieve that program, leading to excessive marijuana consumption into a glazing brain fog and a dissolution to what time is for the rest of us.

The programs also have a lateral framework which connects them like so:

Program One: Infancy<->Program Five: Ecstasy
Program Two: Territory<->Program Six: Mastery
Program Three: Rationality<->Program Seven: Unity
Program Four: Morality<->Program Eight: Singularity

You can imagine unbearable pain as being the low end of Program One and overwhelming pleasure as the high end of Program Five. The low end of Program

Two manifests as depression and the high end of Program Six is when we discontinue that practice in favor of metaprogramming ourselves to be more in line with the reality we desire, alienating us from those who cannot change their reality's channel. The low end of Program Three is when we use rationality for all things and remain trapped by a singular reality tunnel where language, beliefs, and subsequent decisions leave us strapped in to the isolation of our "self." The high end of Program Seven is a state of timeless unity with the cosmos so profound you wouldn't even notice if you were bleeding to death. Lastly, the low end of Program Four is utter adherence to social laws and moral taboos, being so afraid of your own thoughts and worldview that may be contrary to those around you that you conceal them. Whereas the high end of Program Eight is abandoning human morality in favor of what theoretical higher forms have yet to make themselves known, being so "beyond" it all that you would most likely end up institutionalized as you could not sanely live in a society so apart from your own unique metaphysical worldview.

The newer programs should be treaded lightly for they seem to anticipate not ourselves, but what is to come next. This is why dwelling in the high ends of Programs Five to Eight is as wrong-headed as complacently remaining in the low ends of Programs One to Four.

You might also see that yoga and meditation have not exactly been outlawed, and those, of course, are paths to the higher programs. But hasn't toxic culture come to embrace the complete opposite of these notions and ideals? To give organizations your attention before yourself and your dreams? To engage in monotony and plug in to some network where any thought can be acted upon to kill three hours of your life on YouTube?

Question: When, if ever, can you say you've experienced the latter four programs of consciousness? Were they positive experiences or frightening ones? Describe them.

16

"I am 100 percent in favor of the intelligent use of drugs, and 1,000 percent against the thoughtless use of them, whether caffeine or LSD. And drugs are not central to my life."

-Timothy Leary

There is no actual Eight-program system that exists in the brain; we are only modeling everything that can be experienced or may be experienced. The entire system is very abstract, especially the latter four programs, so this chapter will be an attempt to apply some of the information given to what reality I've known in hopes of clarifying things. It's certainly worth a try, but I must urge you to begin studying this model in far greater depth than what I have laid out here and define what's healthy and toxic for yourself on your own.

Often times, I think of how unlikely my existence is and by proxy, this book. I could have easily not been born or never have arrived at these critical thoughts. It was all very slim happenstance that I am deeply grateful for. As you might imagine, I don't see any prophesied greater destiny. I'm just trying to entertain and help others where I may.

I was programmed by my grandmother to be Catholic, but I fell out very young. And not out of skepticism but boredom. I felt no positive feelings from that indoctrinated spirituality, only the fear of punishment from God. Several years later, I developed an atheist streak that informed my teenage years. Later I grew into a more agnostic state. Then when I was eighteen, an even greater shift in my consciousness took place. I think of it as the dissolution of my immorality. At age eighteen, I had a detached retina in my left eye that I ignored for weeks in hope of recovering (after all, I was so strong and young) until it took the people in my life to tell me I needed to go get check out. Turns out my macula was torn, and I would suffer permanent damage to my vision. No glasses, lasers, or contacts would compensate for the damage.

That played out into a long Program Two emotional crisis where I realized the purpose of one part of my body had been ruined to such a degree that it would never function again (I even had to rely on my mother and girlfriend at the time for survival). Then the post-surgery upset my back because I have to lie in an unfamiliar position for weeks, resulting in the most agonizing, persisting pain I've ever experienced in my entire life. Before that time I never truly conceived of entropy or death. I was immortal until that moment. Beyond that, I perceived the reality that if I am only a brain and body, then I'm decaying and there would be much more to come.

As much as I tried to live my life back then, I often faltered into a deep despair. What got me out was the journey of accepting, which included the pursuit of having an out-of-body experience.

I wanted one for the same reason I've always wanted to see a ghost. No matter how terrifying a ghost might be, it would be personal proof that this life is not all there is. I am so glad I became fixed on this path, as though the discoveries were unsettling, that journey has brought me peace of mind and purpose.

No, I've never had an out-of-body experience—what the literal term of "extraterrestrial" means according to Antero Alli, or the experience of Program Eight of consciousness. But that doesn't mean I haven't tried. In fact, I've induced some near-death experiences such as skydiving, that hobby of falling to your death until the last second. Is there some part of us that cannot be carried within our physicality? Some soul or spirit? I have my doubts but would enjoy being proven wrong.

Some of the greatest experiences I've ever had took place in those higher states of consciousness after that question. There were feelings the Catholic Church could never seem give me.

The experiences of being in love, near-death, belonging with a community that cherish your ideals, the effects of *certain* drugs, and culture shock encompass some of the most seminal and vitally extraordinary moments of my life. I have lived well and continue with informed nuance, so if I am mistaken and there is more after death, it is just a bonus round for me.

Trying Ayahuasca was one of my most rewarding

and unique experiences of my life. It largely concluded my quest to apprehend if I possessed a soul. It triggered for me Program Seven consciousness, where nonduality set in, but it also seemed to open my mental energies outward to perceive autonomous entities beyond myself. Certainly angelic, ultra-terrestrial, or even "translinguistic" might fit the bill here, but I subsequently decided it was more likely that those "autonomous entities" were only a sophisticated manifestation of my consciousness and unconscious mind. Could I be wrong? Honestly, I hope so. However, there are severe problems with the interactions between physics and metaphysics, and that's why they're not the same word. Perhaps that is a myopic human convention, but let's talk about ghosts. Corey Taylor (yeah, the guy from Slipknot) actually has a really cool theory he calls the "intelligent energy" idea, that when we die our energy is displaced beyond our body and carries on. Physics supports this in a limited fashion with the Law of Conservation of Energy. After all, the energy a human produces does not just go away. So he says the energy of a strong soul or will carries on and then can interact with other energies, namely other humans or electronics.

This soul energy is not of the same composition as known particles, and this is where I begin to feel something is missing with this idea. That is due to the fact that it also would mean that the energy would have properties of both physical and metaphysical (or at least very least, a kind of matter we haven't detected or decoded such as dark matter) substances. And those sightings of ghosts would then mean these two fundamentally different kinds of substances were interacting, which as you can see creates many issues. Unless you assume that ghosts are autonomous entities and it's all connected, that there is a greater force of intelligence that has harnessed or advanced past known laws of the universe. In any case, that is why we would like to experience the higher states of consciousness. Because if metaphysics and souls are currently both unprovable and false, perhaps they could one day be true.

Question: What was the closest to the most perfect day of your life? What do you think happens to you after death? Have you ever believed otherwise? Have you ever encountered autonomous entities (ghosts, aliens, demons, angels, gods)? If so, why were you visited?

"Do you remember that Looney Tunes cartoon where there's this pathetic coyote who's always chasing and never catching a roadrunner? In pretty much every episode of this cartoon, there's a moment where the coyote is chasing the roadrunner and the roadrunner runs off a cliff, which is fine— he's a bird, he can fly. But the thing is, the coyote runs off the cliff right after him. And what's funny, at least if you're six years old, is that the coyote's totally fine too. He just keeps running — right up until the moment that he looks down and realizes that he's in mid-air. That's when he falls. When we're wrong about something, not when we realize it, but before that, we're like that coyote after he's gone off the cliff and before he looks down. You know, we're already wrong, we're already in trouble, but we feel like we're on solid ground… It does feel like something to be wrong; it feels like being right."

-Kathryn Schulz

Before we wrap up, I feel it is important to discuss the possibility that many of the things stated in this text may go against your beliefs and experience. When I use the word "wrongness," what comes to mind? That is, if something you know is wrong or bad because it's immoral or irrational?

"Wrongness" is a quality no one wishes to possess. The best of us admit when we are shown to be wrong and attempt to better ourselves with the advantage of new information, but most people's ideas of what is right, moral, and actionable are installed early on and never change. Wrongness is harmful enough, specifically because someone who is wrong operates in the exact same manner as one who believes they are right. The brain cannot distinguish between the two states without a heap of contradictory information. It's what Kathryn Schulz calls "error blindness." There is not really a form of wrongness that exists in the present tense in our minds.

For instance, I have always been trying to apply more natural, holistic methods for body care. About ten years ago, I noticed my body was very low on energy a lot of the time. My partner was much healthier: a vegetarian. I began to opt out of unnecessary products. I thought this was made easier by an article on the Internet about the dozens upon of dozens of uses and benefits of coconut oil. The problem is, one of those methods just plain didn't work, yet I believed the article wholeheartedly. So I confidently covered myself in coconut oil one summer day (some years after I'd read the article), feeling rather pleased with myself that I had found a natural sun-screen. Only to discover far too late that, no, coconut oil does not protect your skin against the sun. At least not the kind I used. It was a devastating lesson, but once I realized I was wrong, I knew the folly of my prior faith. We must become humble when recognizing "wrongness" within ourselves and accept any consequences without shame. There is *never* any shame in improvement.

Indeed, all the information given to you in this text is wrong in a certain sense. The concepts of "rightness" and "wrongness" are not absolutes. They are relative to the individual depending on infinite contingencies and circumstances. It's not that Green Day is superior to Weezer (possible evidence including that Weezer covered several Green Day songs over the years and Green Day did not reciprocate). It's that I seem to experience more of an evocation from listening to Green Day than I do Weezer. If you believe the opposite, it doesn't mean I'm wrong, just less in line with your worldview.

This is why the Eight-program model is only a model. It serves to describe the phenomenon of consciousness, but it is not consciousness itself. Someday, a greater method of describing consciousness might become available, if not an outright consensus of a definition for consciousness itself.

Your perspective ought to be as scrutinized as those you oppose. Stop thinking of detractors as evil or ignorant. Toxic culture is personally harmful to our own personal and defined missions, not evil itself. It is to be understood, not attacked.

To circle back to Pirsig's diagnosis from chapter five, that mistake to divide things up into Classic and Romantic methods of thought, it seems Western thought operates under a paradigm that has long been obsolete, but difficult to replace. That is, Aristotelianism. Aristotle was more interested in physical phenomenon than in any unseen world. This was fine in Ancient Greece, but today, modern science urges us to remember the fact that absolute logical syllogisms are no longer useful when we talk about atoms. It's the same argument made previously with E-prime. When we use "is" to describe and equate one thing to another, we are abusing language. This ambiguity can seem screwy at first, until you learn atoms have been proven to be in superposition. That is, both states of an atom are present until the point of observation. And the properties of the atoms are never observed in full, only an aspect of them— never both their speed and position, rather either or.

Robert Pirsig believed in a factual sense, there is no right and wrong. Instead, try replacing "right" or "wrong" with "more advantageous" and "less advantageous" to the context the given situation. Aristotle's logic and physics aren't wrong, but less advantageous than Newton's.

There's an outstanding episode of *It's Always Sunny in Philadelphia* where the gang gets into an argument about evolution. Mac puts on a presentation, which, for all its rhetoric and nonsense, illustrates my point. The presentation is called, "Science Is a Liar Sometimes." It shows that truth (at least human truth) seems to be a function of time.

Even the most cutting edge and empirically verified science will at some point be obsolete. For the most part academia assimilates this new data for its further projects with reasonable gusto. Society and individuals take much longer.

There are numerous objections and detractors to climate change. One popular objection describes how the poles are shifting independent of human intervention, and therefore, whatever climate change is occurring is a result of that, not anything we have done.

Even if this was proven to be unanimously true overnight, it would not change the fact that our current agriculture practices are unsustainable. That the production and wasteful distribution of plastic into our oceans have been found in an alarming number of marine lives. This mode of consumption, if not course corrected, will result in unfounded and irreversible harm. First for the ecosystem at large, lastly for those who denied the data.

Applying the lessons in this text are more challenging given the stubbornness of human conviction. After all, as most people are not metaprogrammers, they have no concern for the world at large. They are instead concerned with themselves or their immediate pack. Thus reason, given in even the most convincing argument might not allow for permanent change.

The point is, these ideas are subject to change, even with the changing of my own admitted biases. At this time, the synthesis of these lessons seems to be what people have been after, though they may not find them desirable. Regardless, though the world will remain determined to be absurd, you have the option not to be.

Culturally, the United States consumes meat in veracious excess. To challenge this status quo is heretical to nationalists. Industry represents the ideals of what America stands for. Part of that industry, to survive, involves suppressing scientific research that shows what ways its practices are harmful. It's why climate change is up for debate, even though the evidence is overwhelmingly on the side of our needing to make adjustments.

On the bright side, Dr. Michael Greger does compare eating meat today to cigarette smoking in the 1950's, because doctors didn't preach on the health risks and so people did it without understanding the consequences. The next few generations might latch on and adapt, but will it be too late? What actions does an activist have when it seems hopeless? If rationality is not effective, what else can we use?

Briefly consider the ethics of a religion that espoused unconditional worship of the planet. Using the ideals of the divine and supernatural to coax people into believing things for the greater good. After all, the divine has been used to coax people into believing things that were not for the greater good. It's as difficult to change your own mind as it is to change others.

So how committed are you to your ideals? Or would you call yourself a person with convictions? A set of values and core beliefs? There's a big difference between the words of commitment and conviction.

One of them has a very positive connotation. If you're committed to the people in your life, most would consider that a likable quality. Conviction has a very negative connotation. Is it important to have convictions, even if it means you might die for them? Perhaps, when something greater is at stake. An individual life is not anywhere near as valuable as an ideal. A person can embody an ideal, still contain a personality, and yet the magnitude of that ideal is greater than the single person in question. This is because it is our thoughts that unite us the most. If we were ever to unite under one ideology, there would be an incredibly powerful and permanent altering of our destiny. What if this ideal was in existence? Surely that is a possibility, if one likes to make assumptions. If this ideal was theoretically out there, it is obviously not sufficient for the entire world to collaborate in a new way. Why? Well, if you identify what *you* think that is, the answer is clear. There are innumerable arguments against it and thus the argument becomes the point. Never the ideal itself. And once you're convinced, you don't question your belief. Belief systems are the foundation of faith.

If you're committed to something, you won't abandon it lightly. Nor would you be content to let it be tarnished unfairly. When you have a conviction, it is relatively indelible. Pervasive, consuming. At this level, the mind would sooner end than betray that convicted thing. I've heard many anecdotes of people trying to build Earthships in communities only to be consistently shut down by the local municipalities.

In other cases, an ideology gains so much energy and individuals that violence could be warranted— on one side or the other. The fact is any person could be thrust into violence and murder given the conditions. To exist is a challenge and a threat to others in many scenarios. What I desire is to curb the point of conviction for anything. E-prime is a great tool for that, but you might understand why it has not been implemented at large. People don't want to give up what they feel about their bodies, egos, and destinies.

The main theme of the Dragon Ball series is progression through struggle. I think that's such a vital lesson to learn and a very important theme to cling to. You find that, as you're improving, the barrier to what you want likewise increases as well. Some people proceed despite this. It gets so bad that their ideologies get challenged and contested in a court of law. It could be something so severe that you're perceived to be against the standing societal order. Like Michael Reynolds seeing the need for sustainable housing test sites. Then there's the case of Rob Potylo.

Potylo had a web series that was optioned for television: after a major network signed a contract, they dropped him, reneging on the show. Both men were peons in the cogs of the machine: it was the power of their ideals that triumphed then. It's tragic, but this doesn't always happen. See, when it does, it's all the more important to point out. Through great strain on their own part they maintained conviction and refused to let a higher power be what devoured their dreams. As a result, they both won (Reynolds got his site and Potylo settled out of court with an appreciable compensation). They didn't know if they really stood a chance. That's not what mattered. What mattered was that obstinacy. The proof of how progression through struggle can work!

Progression through struggle does not mean putting yourself through survival situations on behalf of your convictions. It is the commitment of meeting your life in accordance with reality to achieve a more conductive state of consciousness.

Is the title of this book meant to oppose to the Alt-right? Well no, not exclusively. Though we have spent plenty of time criticizing that white nationalist mindset, we must also try to accept the fact that most of that group is acting out of the basic mammalian fear of tribal invasion; cultural erasure or being threatened out of a certain social stature due to a change in power dynamics or enacted equality. A lower consciousness preoccupation of territory being threatened! There is no debate to be found with the idea that the world is not as it ought to be. But also that if we accept it as it is, we are willing an inextinguishable harm to come.

With metaprogramming, one will find a remedy to the reality tunnel of the Alt-right. It is meant to collapse our disparate views, to synthesize a solution. The idea behind the alternative wrong is on the surface a rhetorical response to my country's politics in the past few years. The Alt-right is an alternative to American

Conservatism embodying racial elitism, consumerism, and toxic masculinity, but they are a tiny subsection of many other nuanced groups, issues, and positions previously called out here.

The phrase "the alternative wrong" denotes that very notion within the self: that feeling of being right, although you are not. That psychological trick our minds play in that discovery and its subsequent decision that you are always responsible to either carry on with the error or improve upon it… the weight of that is what must be embraced.

New Orleans is one of those cities covered in graffiti. It seems to have risen with the abandoning of the many buildings and limited avenues for creative expression. There is one common motif you find in various parts of the city. A sign that says, "Think that you might be wrong."

I fear the person who would dispute that. Sometimes you *will* be mistaken.

Instead of denial, shame, or despair— find a way to grow. The alternative wrong means to do something *right* when faced with your mistakes. Take responsibility and do better, *compassionately*.

Question: Frame everything you disagree with in this text in terms of E-prime. Instead of stating I am wrong about "X." Say, "It seems to me that you're wrong based on the following information I have access to at the time, which is…" You might need to not only cite some sources but check them with more scrutiny than you ever have before. Now perhaps you can see how emotions power the majority of your decisions and beliefs. How does that make you feel? As I close this text, I want it to be known that part my own belief system is that I believe my beliefs are very malleable and I am open to factual information to change or improve my views. Are you?

18

"If there is one lesson we can learn from our history, it is that humanity, when faced with life-threatening crises, has risen to the challenge and has reached for even higher goals. In some sense, the spirit of exploration is in our genes and hardwired into our soul. But now we face perhaps the greatest challenge of all: to leave the confines of the Earth and soar into outer space. The laws of physics are clear; sooner or later we will face global crises that threaten our very existence."

-Michio Kaku

No matter who you are or what you believe, there is no arguing that getting people their basest needs met is paramount. People need to know and strive for them specifically. From there, every human could hypothetically start shifting the evolutionary process into a manual rather than an automatic position. Life and evolution seem to seek nothing less than the abolishment of entropy and chaos. There's no doubt you've contemplated these ideas previously. What will be our fate?

In ancient times, it's as simple as the Buddha's teachings to be liberated from the three snakes of greed, ignorance, and anger. When you have your needs met, you can start addressing others. When humanity has all of its needs met, we might learn something hitherto unknown. If human sexuality is no longer a taboo or "solely for reproduction," the shift would be so great it would beckon an alternative purpose for humanity. This would run counter to the majority process of simply growing up, giving birth and dying. The needs of existing children could be labeled as a priority. In Plato's Republic, it was suggested that an ideal utopian society would have no individualized parenting. Instead, everyone raised the children collectively, relatively unsure of which one was theirs. Though that was a harsh mandate in the Republic, it could be starting today. With genetic engineering, it will become more and more common to pass on traditional birth in favor of more convenient and advanced methods. In that, ideally, no one would be punished for desiring a traditional birth, but the process may simply fall out of fashion for future humans. It's around this point in our hypothetical future that I think philosophic love will begin to flourish for us all.

Now onto the ideal case for our arrival into the Technological Singularity, which is merging our human consciousness with artificial intelligence: extended intelligence. If the Technological Singularity is going to take place, it would be best if the world sentient robots entered into wasn't one it wanted to destroy. Now, if the idea of robots surpassing human intelligence and dominating us still seems far-fetched to you, I can sympathize.

Think of the Internet as a very early symptom of

this coming event. An extremely proto-hive mind. The mecha anime *Neon Genesis Evangelion* seems to be a loose playing-out of this event. The climax of the series brings all living beings back into a state of oneness known as the Human Instrumentality Project, where the borders between beings dissolve and individuality is null. There is only void. The show was released in 1995, and yet the Human Instrumentality Project seems to have a lot of parallels to the Internet. People dissolving into a different world where the barriers between people are a little less defined. Phrases, languages, and memes are transcending borders.

The main character comes to reject this state of existence, even though the show's mythology states it is how all of life began and ought to return. When the Internet became a household idea, no one could predict how social dynamics would be forever altered. Asking what was going to be changed, gained, and lost was not a conversation that was had until after the shift had taken place.

I have difficulty in believing the Technological Singularity could happen, but the trend of knowledge it either will continue to grow exponentially and thus produce something much more evolved than Homo sapiens, or the acceleration will level off. This second scenario would be upsetting because it would mean either civilization was wiped out or some kind of idiocracy that catered to the short-term needs of selfishness and ignorance would prevail.

Michael Reynolds wrote: "How far will we be able to go? How far do we want to go? We have not begun to realize the potential of this thing called consciousness in the human condition. Will consciousness reveal itself as an entity without need of a body? Are there more major leaps and transformations ahead?... To take these bodies— these dogmas— to the heavens is absurd. You wouldn't take your house with you on a trip around the world, so why must we take the human form on a trip around the universe? We are not trapped in our house. Or are we? We are not trapped in our bodies. Or are we?"

Traditional Buddhism refuses the concept of self, and this is to emphasize that the human condition would not be able to intuit the fact that each thing is one Thing. A computer is the Buddha in drag. The self is not the Internet, but all ego is slowly being digitized, converted from organic consciousness to inorganic silicon and whatever must come after (be it quantum or molecular computer), gaining a new more tangible degree of physicality that lends a simpler line of questioning to the greatest philosophical inquiries of all time. Consequently, the mystique of the universe will be potentially accessible as never was before. That or it will be accepted as unknowable and therefore, no longer worth further energy. In the meantime, may my body outlast the damaging frailty of ego— concern over my image, standing in my species, and dissatisfaction with my own existence.

The fantasy epic *A Song of Ice and Fire* has

preternatural antagonists known as White Walkers. They are the true threat facing the feuding characters in that story, yet the protagonists constantly fight amongst themselves. It is an allegory for the real world. Racism, industrialism, and certain technologies are all threats that could easily lead to global devastation tomorrow. Humanity must unite and defeat its White Walkers, and it is very capable of doing so. Notice how often the world could end yet doesn't.

If this overcoming takes place, some futurists anticipate hostile artificial intelligence. But let's say human augmentation does occur. Using robots to better our biology. It is more likely to produce new schisms—fear from the advent of human genetic, robotic, and nanobot manipulation. Biblically savvy folks would probably consider those things unnatural and even Mark of the Beast Rapture kind of things. It could get violent. Many fundamentalists and naturalists would resort to severe measures to prevent this augmentation from becoming commonplace, even perhaps terrorism. Death threats against immortality. How curious.

Barring that and continuing to speculate, our reality has been authored by DNA. Our brains are reaching a kind of computational limit in terms of hardware and we are not physically evolving to reflect the booming developments of knowledge. This is why, as time goes on, the amount of information a person is able to learn is relatively limited, while the amount of information available is not. Fields of study are now extremely deep and specified. The precursor to integration with sentient artificial intelligence would be body augmentation such as nanobots or microcomputers in our brains that would store accessible information. Think Google but without the middle man of a device. These kinds of gadgets are being developed. Objects not only for more efficient thought but also synthetic organs and skin to better maintain or replace our aging ones. Artificial human life extension and human intelligence enhancement. These futurists are even optimistic enough to say our generation may solve the problem of dying.

As awesome as all that sounds, what good is immortality if people remain involved with famine, war, and suffering? Yes, these developments are promising, but a futurist's priority should be clean water and energy to the entire planet.

So then, if all goes well, we're destined to become metaprogrammers. As we move forward, it's going to be something we'll all be able to do. We won't even have to read books or learn about it; it'll be an augmented consciousness within us. Wired to favor this specific type of intentional development and erode away self-defeating and self-harming ideas. Or automatically rendered psychological imprinting. This is why we must be weary and perform metaprogramming competently on our own, so that the result isn't just another great advancement for the pacification of a miserable populous. We now know how malleable personality and identity really are. Let's not allow this knowledge to continue to hold ourselves back as people; we must take control of our minds now before someone else does. The worst of all dystopian nightmares would be the world programmed, but by the elite, turning our freedom into an "obsolete" program and wiring us to serve once and for all. This is why it is so important that you become whoever you want to be in this moment. Waiting for tomorrow or a better future is not going to cut it.

You know now new forms of consciousness will be reached. Transgender people will perhaps be able to inhabit whether form they most desire, whether as in avatar in virtual reality or a synthetic body in the real world. It will all have started with the group insisting that there are more than two genders. Age will become more commonly divided into biological and genetic, that is, how old is your body versus how much have you actually aged? Social and genetic scripts initiated at the dawn of life on Earth will be revised.

We're on track to outgrow Earth. And not because we've destroyed it because we needed fossil fuels and hamburgers, but because it won't be a big enough playground for us. The galaxy is waiting.

And then what and then what and then what?

That's really up to your imagination. Here's what I'm hoping for, though— finding a way to break the speed of light. See, if we can do that, we can colonize and inhabit not only our galaxy, but the entire universe. If we can't, then we're pretty much stuck where we are because space is that vast. But let's say we can, all right? Then we evolve upon our own evolution that evolved upon itself. It's no longer Homo sapiens. We'd be much more space-worthy and evolving apart from our prior symbiosis to Earth. Actually, it would be so incomprehensible to us, you might as well call it God or Krishna or whatever. That's the entire point of Hegel's philosophy. He saw history as the progress of consciousness to the point of divinity. Robert Pirsig would consider it moving toward a state of Dynamic Quality, good as a noun. Cosmologist Frank Tippler referred to it as the Omega Point. The area of space-time where our being is so darn advanced it is what we'd now consider God. A being not subject to linear time or inevitable death. A hive mind of benevolence, driven by humanity's motivation to hack our own programming onto an approaching perfection.

Is this projected future of humanity ideal or even desirable, though? From what I have gathered, these speculations are the best-case scenario. The end of man. There must not be hubris in beckoning the next step.

According to biologists, all life on Earth was once one. The nondualist concept is hard to grasp for any individual consciousness, but at some point in the past, it was so. Our course seems to be a possible returning to that ideal: Nirvana, Heaven, Eternity. A return, but an improvement— less but better. The project of evolution evolving. My explanation just uses human progress as the catalyst for divinity. The hero's journey coming back to where they began, having changed.

Thus, we must spread and apply the information

here, but most importantly the concept of metaprogramming. Laws can be made to diminish consciousness change or brainwash the population, but human law cannot separate the mind from its desire, its ability, to free itself.

Question: Has your view of who you are been challenged and/or changed since reading this text? In what ways? What, in your mind, are the limits of humanity? How far will we be able to go? Will we transcend the speed of light? Would you even consider us human at that point?

19

"People today distinguish between knowing and acting and pursue them separately, believing that one must know before one can act. They will discuss and learn the business of knowledge first, they say, and wait till they truly know before they put their knowledge into practice. Consequently, to the last days of life, they will never act and also never know. This doctrine of knowing first and acting later is not a minor disease and it did not come about yesterday. My present advocacy of the unity of knowing and acting is precisely the medicine for that disease."

-Wangyang Ming

No book is for everyone, and because toxic is an abstract buzz word, I have no doubt some people will argue I am espousing some toxic or impractical ideas myself. Time will test my words more harshly than you ever could. That is also why though I write of certain issues passionately or rationally, I'm not trying to tell you what to do. I'm telling you what things might improve if you chose to of your own volition. To that end, I would call together those who wished to carry on the words here, whether that is to refute or to spread or to question. Though I'm not much of a debater. These ideas and intentions for life are meant as suggestions, though they have been extensively proven to give one more agency and control in one's own life time and time again (hence the appendix so you can read upon greater minds than mine).

Though the way is wrought with peril, my hope is this work has opened up a point in your heart or your mind and can see where I'm coming from. I believe you can be even better. Just make sure you have fun on the way there!

If you're curious of how to train yourself to become a metaprogrammer, understand I haven't shown you here, plus I would hope you would first ease into the various ideologies of consciousness change and expansion lest you go awry as Nietzsche did. This was just me showing you the "candy" you get from playing with this model of consciousness. What you do next is on you. I do not believe the visions in this text are mere dreams. It is imperative that we do not let the state of the world overwhelm us. Our aim is the moral activity that comes with the alternative wrong. Become debt-free. Form a covenant with nature by experiencing an Earthship or another off-the-grid housing. Free yourself from the indoctrination of your family, your culture, your default reality tunnel if only to see if there is a better way of going about things. Put yourself in a position where you can be proven wrong. Live with passion by seeking love, creativity, and adventure. Laugh so hard you can't breathe. Utilize the practice of metaprogramming to become self-sufficient and tame your mind's consciousness for fun, profit, and fulfillment. Then spread this starting point to every person you know.

The reason why we define ourselves in different ways is because each of our experiences seems to greatly differ. The things we've been through ultimately shape us, but there is always an opportunity to refuse to be defined simply by our experiences.

So many traditions are dead cultural ideas in need of uprooting for the benefit of the next generation. When they are consumed, they provide us with the toxicity we experience, for they are rotten! Recycle them, compost them, and build a rational wall around the heart of them! The prime example of this is what Leary and others did with the creation of the Eight-program model. They took something that was esoteric and made it evident.

I see people in one of four states in life— surviving, struggling, struggling well, and thriving. Wherever you currently feel you stand, my earnest hope is with the tools for consciousness change I've provided you, you can beckon your ascension— for there is a wonderful place in the whole of humanity for all people within to thrive. It's found in the most cherished memories of your life and the center of all the humans needs: a sensation that hopes to counter that selfishness so powerful it could end us all— but not before casting decades of misery and regret upon those we would bequeath this world to.

Be feisty, but patient. Taking control of your existence, your health, and your future *can* be done. Just because it should have happened yesterday, that doesn't mean it can't happen now. Be grateful. Whatever you are now wasn't entirely your decision.

Whatever you want to be will be now.

A. Source Material & Further Reading for Consciousness Correction

Part One

James, William. *The Essential William James*. Prometheus Books, 2011.

1

"The Universe and Beyond, with Stephen Hawking." *StarTalk Radio Show by Neil DeGrasse Tyson*, www.startalkradio.net/show/universe-beyond-stephen-hawking/

2

Wilson, Robert Anton. *Prometheus Rising*. New Falcon Publications, 2016.

Malaclypse, and Kerry W. Thornley. *Principia Discordia, or, How I Found Goddess and What I Did to Her When I Found Her*. Paladin Press, 2014.

3

Sartre, Jean-Paul. *The Transcendence of the Ego: an Existential Theory of Consciousness*. Routledge, 2004.

Leary, Timothy. Info-Psychology: a Manual on the Use of the Human Nervous System According to the Instructions of the Manufacturers and a

Navigational Guide for Piloting the Evolution of the Human Individual. New Falcon Publications, 2011.

Wilson, Robert Anton. *Prometheus Rising*. New Falcon Publications, 2016.

Basic Writings of Nietzsche: Birth of Tragedy: Beyond Good and Evil: On the Genealogy of Morals: Ecce Homo, by Friedrich Wilhelm Nietzsche and Walter Kaufmann, Modern Library, 1968.

4

Kurzweil, Ray. *The Singularity Is Near: When Humans Transcend Biology*. Duckworth, 2016.

Baum, Dan. "Legalize It All: How To Win The War on Drugs." *Harper's Magazine*, 31 Mar. 2016, harpers.org/archive/2016/04/legalize-it-all/.

Doblin, R. "Dr. Leary's Concord Prison Experiment: a 34-Year Follow-up Study." *Journal of Psychoactive Drugs*, U.S. National Library of Medicine, 1998, www.ncbi.nlm.nih.gov/pubmed/9924845.

Part Two

Final Fantasy X. Squaresoft. 2001.

5

Pirsig, Robert M. *Zen and the Art of Motorcycle Maintenance: an Inquiry into Values*. Vintage Books, 2014.

Heede, Richard. "Tracing Anthropogenic Carbon Dioxide and Methane Emissions to Fossil Fuel and Cement Producers, 1854–2010." *Climatic Change*, vol. 122, no. 1-2, 2013, pp. 229–241.

Pirsig, Robert M. *Lila: an Inquiry into Morals: Robert M. Pirsig*. Black Swan, 1993.

6

Reynolds, Michael E. *A Coming of Wizards: a Manual of Human Potential*. High Mesa Foundation, 1989.

Garbage Warrior. Directed by Oliver Hodge. 2007.

Carroll, Ryder. *The Bullet Journal Method Track Your Past, Order Your Present, Plan Your Future*. 4th Estate, 2018.

7

Hodes, John. "Evolutionary Origins of Homosexuality." *The Gay & Lesbian Review*, 7 Mar. 2018, glreview.org/article/evolutionary-origins-of-homosexuality/.

Bourland, D. David, and Paul Dennithorne Johnston. *To Be or Not: an E-Prime Anthology*. International Society for General Semantics, 1991.

8

Robbins, Tony. "Ultimate Edge." *Tonyrobbins.com*, www.tonyrobbins.com/ultimate-edge/.

Leary, Timothy. *Turn on, Tune in, Drop Out*. Ronin, 2001.

9

Teixeira, Diana. "United Nations Office on Drugs and Crime." *World Drug Report 2018: Opioid Crisis, Prescription Drug Abuse Expands; Cocaine and Opium Hit Record Highs*, www.unodc.org/unodc/en/frontpage/2018/June/world-drug-report-2018_-opioid-crisis--prescription-drug-abuse-expands-cocaine-and-opium-hit-record-highs.html.

Greger, Michael. *How Not to Die*. Pan Books, 2017.

10

Sadamoto, Yoshiyuki. *Neon Genesis Evangelion*. Viz Media, 2013.

11

Campbell, Joseph, and Bill D. Moyers. *The Power of Myth*. Library of Congress, NLS/BPH, 1989.

Hegel, Georg Wilhelm Friedrich, et al. *Hegel's Phenomenology of Spirit*. Oxford University Press, 1994.

Schopenhauer, Arthur, and E. F. J. Payne. *The World as Will and Representation*. Dover Publications, 1966.

Sartre, Jean-Paul. *Being and Nothingness: a Phenomenological Ontology*. Washington Square Press, 1972.

Schmidt, JK. *Rick And Morty Co-Creator Dan Harmon Questions The Meaning Of Life*. ComicBook.com, 5 Sept. 2017, comicbook.com/tv-shows/2017/06/07/rick-and-morty-creator-dan-harmon-questions-the-meaning-of-life/.

12

Watts, Alan W. *Wisdom Of Insecurity: a Message for an Age of Anxiety*. Ebury Digital, 2012.

Patanjali, and Alistair Shearer. *The Yoga Sutras of Patanjali*. Bell Tower, 2002.

Wallis, Christopher D. *Tantra Illuminated: the Philosophy, History, and Practice of a Timeless Tradition*. Mattamayuˉra Press, 2013.

13

Truant, Johnny B. *The Bialy Pimps*. Realm & Sands. 2012.

Hyatt, Christopher S. *Secrets of Western Tantra: the Sexuality of the Middle Path*. Original Falcon Press, 2010.

14

Salzberg, Sharon. *Real Happiness: The Power of Meditation*. Workman Publishing, 2011.

Part Three

15

Alli, Antero, and Robert Anton Wilson. *Angel Tech: a Modern Shaman's Guide to Reality Selection*. Original Falcon Press, 2012.

16

Taylor, Corey. *A Funny Thing Happened On The Way To Heaven*. Random House UK, 2014.

17

Schulz, Kathryn. *Being Wrong: Adventures in the Margin of Error*. HarperCollins, 2011.

Faraone, Chris, et al. "Desperation Wins." *DigBoston*, 21 Feb. 2017, digboston.com/ desperation-wins/.

18

Kaku, Michio. *The Future of Humanity: Terraforming Mars, Interstellar Travel, Immortality and Our Destiny beyond Earth.* Penguin Books, 2019.

Thank you SO MUCH for reading this book!!!

If you enjoyed it, I do hope you'll leave a review on this book's Amazon page. As an indie author, I cannot understate the importance of reviews. They pretty much determine whether or not I can continue producing more content and get it out to you in an orderly fashion. On top of that, they allow me to improve the way I do things and create even greater stories. If you're interested in receiving a free review copy of any of my other titles, leave an honest review for this book where you purchased it. Send a link of your review to ryansleavittscifi@gmail.com. I'll smile, and send the next book of your choice right over!

I have a lot of interesting stuff coming soon. You can sign-up for my newsletter at:

www.ryansleavitt.com

Earth is gone… humanity is not.

A cutting-edge sci-fi serial about the desperate preservation of life, consciousness, and love in the wake of Earth's end.

Is it worse to learn or not to know?

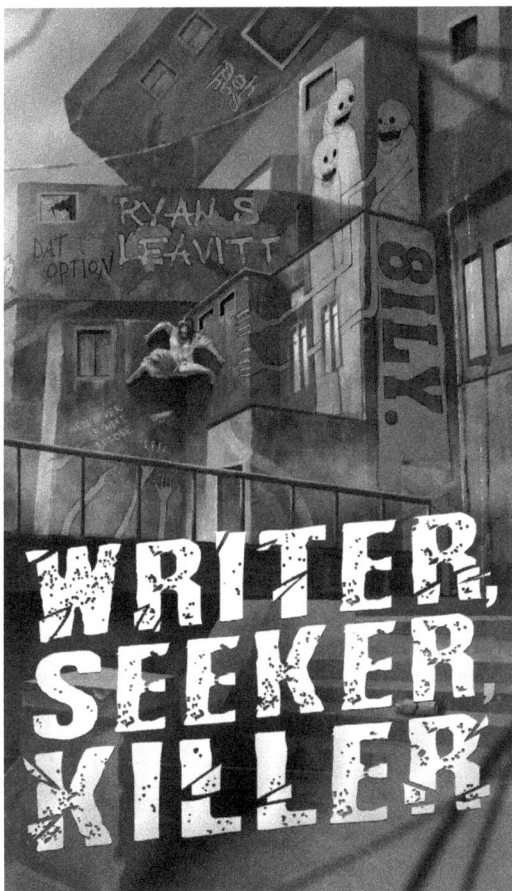

A psychological thriller set in New Orleans
dealing with the failure of the War on Drugs
and a search for the metaphysical.

About the Author

Ryan Starbloak is an author, who also writes under the name Ryan S. Leavitt. His books have been featured on BookBub and he has also appeared on the briefly televised reality sitcom *Quiet Desperation*. He currently lives in New Orleans, where he also performs in the bands Allision and The Every Year.

Instagram: @theeveryyear
Youtube: Ryan S. Leavitt
Music: allision.bandcamp.com
theeveryyear.bandcamp.com